Personalized PD:

Flipping Your Professional Development

THE
Bretzmann
GROUP

NEW BERLIN, WISCONSIN

Personalized PD: Flipping Your Professional Development

The Bretzmann Group, LLC
jbretzmann@bretzmanngroup.com
www.bretzmanngroup.com

Publisher: Jason Bretzmann
Copy Editor: Cory Peppler
Cover Designer: Kelly M. Kurtz
Project Coordinator: Kenny Bosch

First Edition
ISBN: 0692483322
ISBN-13: 978-0692483329
Printed in the United States of America

Also published by The Bretzmann Group, LLC:
Flipping 2.0: Practical Strategies for Flipping Your Class
Available in print at tinyurl.com/flipping20 and
on your Kindle at tinyurl.com/flipping20k

Dedication

To those tireless, energizing, constantly-learning teachers who work hard every day to teach our kids. To the professional educators who are also intense learners who explore ideas, information, and tools on their own on a daily basis. To those administrators and coaches who have worked alongside others to differentiate, individualize, and personalize learning. This book is a guidebook for places you have already been. We look forward to sharing the next journeys with you.

And to the friends and families who support and encourage our constant learning as educators. Thank you for giving us the space to learn more, move forward, and share what we know.

Most importantly thank you to Chris Bretzmann, and Jack and Cooper. Thank you to Katie Bosch, Madeline, Kenneth, and Sophia.

We love you all.

Jason Bretzmann and Kenny Bosch

Contents

A Letter from the Cybrary Man

Dear Educator,

After teaching for twenty years in the New York City school system, I was asked by my principal to take over the library program in our middle school. In 1999, I created a library website for the students, parents, and staff of the school. In order to accomplish this, I taught myself HTML. I am self-taught, and I would love to see students and educators take the initiative to learn on their own and not wait for professional development to come to them. In today's digital world, you can learn just about anything you want—and in most cases for free—if you know where to search for it.

When I retired, I decided to expand the original site to include information for all grade levels and most subject areas. Since I am a constant learner and want to keep up with the latest, I am constantly collecting more sites to add to my collection. My global PLN (Personalized Learning Network) on Twitter provides me with excellent educational resources.

We need to teach children how to be responsible citizens, learn to evaluate the information they find, curate valuable resources, and then share them with others.

Cybrary Man's Educational Web Site cybraryman.com is an attempt to provide students, parents, and educators with a one-stop site for finding information. I hope you find it useful in your personalized learning process.

Sincerely,

Jerry Blumengarten
@cybraryman1 on Twitter

Foreword

Personalizing professional development is one of the most transformational shifts in teacher training and school leadership today. The teachers we hire derive from different backgrounds and experiences, and the diversity and knowledge they bring to all of our schools increases the positive power of our school communities. It is a commonly held belief that no two teachers learn the exact same way, yet we have we been providing one-size-fits-all learning for teachers. In *Personalized PD: Flipping Your Professional Development*, the authors show us how good teaching and personalized learning are not just necessary in the classroom, but also in our staff meetings and teacher trainings. Our teachers need opportunities to collaborate and communicate with their colleagues to grow as professionals. A personalized approach to teacher development will lead to more effective PD sessions, increased high-level instruction, and student success. I firmly believe that excellent teachers will move ordinary children to do extraordinary things!

Successful schools have recognized that more personalized instruction for students is paramount to their success, and we need to approach professional development for our teachers with the same enthusiasm and passion! Personalized professional development for school and district leaders will help us to become more comfortable with providing teachers the opportunities to drive their own learning and development. Teachers will become more confident in their use of technology and social media when we become more comfortable with infusing our professional development with the same tools and strategies. Everyone in the school must innovate, disrupt norms, and take risks daily. I often say to my staff and audiences around the world that PD is not only professional development; it is personal development as well.

So why did Jason Bretzmann and his co-authors choose to write a book focusing on personalized PD? They are smart enough to know that resilient and courageous school leaders need to make bold decisions, and create a culture in schools where professional development and personalized learning are respected. When teachers understand and embrace personalized learning, they will welcome the opportunity to be exposed to continuous, high quality, and relevant personalized PD. The authors are absolutely on-point when they say our goal should be to encourage teachers to take risks each day, challenge the status quo, and become innovative to ensure all students achieve their dreams. But we must first show our teachers the respect they deserve and trust them to learn from their experiences. Give students and teachers the autonomy to be creative and "out of the box" thinkers. Our teachers should be encouraged to engage in education chats on twitter, attend EdCamps and conferences, make presentations in flipped staff meetings, and seek to participate in joint PD sessions with other schools and districts.

As the principal, I must give my teachers the time and opportunity to participate in peer observations and receive meaningful feedback in a timely manner. The experienced teachers in our schools who are innovative and creative can have a tremendous influence on the ones just coming into our awesome profession. Much of the expertise we need can be found in our own school buildings and districts. School and district leaders will need to provide the time and resources for teachers to maximize the learning opportunities personalized PD will present. This may mean changing school schedules to accommodate PLC meetings, managing budgets to support continuous job-embedded PD for staff ,and offering an extended day or year to provide flexible opportunities for professional development. One of the best things a school leader can do for his or her teachers is help them to improve their practice. Transformational leaders shift mindsets and inspire others to do the same. *Personalized PD: Flipping Your Professional Development* will give everyone the blueprint to inspire change in our schools and the way that we train our staffs. After reading this book, you will feel empowered and motivated to flip your professional development and personalize learning for your teachers and students. If we listen to the authors, we will be on our way to improving our school cultures and fostering a positive school climate so teachers and leaders can focus on the protective processes that build resilience in all of our students.

Salome Thomas-EL ("Principal EL")
July 2015
www.PrincipalEL.com
Wilmington, Delaware

PERSONALIZED PD:

Flipping Your Professional Development

Personalized PD:
A Teacher's Perspective (Part 1)
Jason Bretzmann

When I first read Kristin Daniels' rough draft of her chapter on flipping professional development for the book *Flipping 2.0: Practical Strategies for Flipping Your Class*, I nodded along as I read and proclaimed to my family sitting nearby that what I was reading was awesome. I told them that she gets it. I read a few more pages, and told the family that I was energized and inspired. *This is the way professional development should be*, I said. Then I wrote the same thing on the document I was reading. I don't know if it was a message to Kristin, a mental bookmark for me, or a request to the PD gods to send something better down to us from on high.

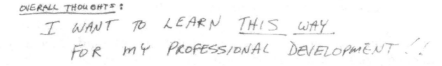

OVERALL THOUGHTS:
I WANT TO LEARN THIS WAY FOR MY PROFESSIONAL DEVELOPMENT!!

Jason's comments on Kristin Daniels' rough draft in Flipping 2.0

What was so profound to me was that Kristin was taking each teacher at their individual starting point and helping them move forward. She found out where they were, asked where they wanted to go, and worked with them to figure out ways to get them there. Sometimes this happened by grouping teachers together who had similar needs. Sometimes it included making videos. Sometimes it was individual conversations and explanations. Sometimes even a large group presentation. However she accomplished it, the bottom line is that it was individualized, and it was ongoing. It was about making constant progress, and it honored the professionals she was working with. It was energizing, and it included opportunities to collaborate and share. These are six good, unifying factors for most professional development.

Benchmarks Should Be Benched

As teachers who have been victims of standardized professional development, we say benchmarks should be benched.

Here's the problem (especially in the world of educational technology). When a school or district sets a standard, however well-meaning, they lose or alienate just about everybody they are trying to move forward. Little or no progress is made. When the same goal is set for everyone, the person who is way behind it thinks, *Well, I'll never get there, so what's the point in trying.* The person already at the benchmark thinks, *Great, I don't have to learn or do a thing. I'm done.* And the person who is well beyond the benchmark concludes, *There is never anything provided for me in this district. I have to learn and do everything on my own.*

Nobody's happy. Some people are upset. Few are learning or innovating. Everyone is stagnant or worse. Instead of the intentional progress being made at the direction of the PD leaders, progress is accidental and sporadic. The individuals who have the PD inflicted upon them are not inspired, and may run the risk of being demoralized. *They really thought I needed to learn THAT?*

Just because we set a benchmark, we shouldn't be fooled into thinking that progress is happening. Just because we provided "something," we shouldn't assume that teachers (and ultimately students) are getting what they need. Similarly, we shouldn't determine that just because we said something everybody learned it. Let's not let ourselves off the hook by checking the box and claiming victory just because we mentioned it at a staff meeting.

There are many remarkable individuals who are learning, connecting, and innovating even though it isn't happening through what is provided. Even so, we want our professional development to happen *because* of what we do, not *in spite* of it.

As educators we can do better than that.

We Could All Tell Stories of the Worst PD

What's the worst professional development you've been a part of (or more accurately: "apart" of)? I'm guessing that your horror stories include things you didn't care about, things you weren't interested in, or things you didn't need for your students. I'm guessing it was a one-time event provided by somebody you didn't know on a topic that you didn't relate to. You may have felt that your time was wasted (or more likely, you did something more productive while the PD was happening).

I remember an award-winning news journalist explaining to the full district staff that he was not an accomplished speaker, and then proving his point over the next hour and a half. Another guy played the banjo and sang songs about death. Still another extolled the virtues of writing across the curriculum, but gave no practical advice on how to do it in the classroom even when she was directly questioned about it. Still another gave several presentations months apart. Each time she claimed to be "under the weather" which was presumably to explain away the fact that her presentations were neither engaging or useful. We could all tell stories.

It's not that their ideas were inherently bad ideas. It's that they didn't provide each teacher, or even groups of teachers with what they needed. They treated everyone the same, and gave nobody what they needed. They were presenter-centric as opposed to audience-centric. Maybe there shouldn't be an audience at all. Maybe everyone should be actively involved in their own individualized process instead of watching from the safety of the comfy chairs.

Of course, there are times when we have to do things we don't want to. I get that. Sometimes there are topics that we need everybody to hear. I get that. There are even times that the best way to learn is in small or even large groups. I get that. Nevertheless, there has got to be a better way to deliver that content.

Hopefully throughout this book, we'll provide some ideas to help get us there. Of course, you should only use what you need, and what can work for you. It would be hypocritical to expect that everything will fit for you. That would be contrary to the premise of this book!

And while I think it's important to bring up and describe the problems, I think it is infinitely more important to work toward solutions. Let's try.

Can We Differentiate?

Standardized PD is akin to the math teacher starting the year with an hour-long lecture on the Pythagorean Theorem. Some students are trying to remember how to do simple algebra, some are tuned out because they already learned this last year, and a third group is wondering when they will ever get to apply their knowledge since this class seems to be going backwards.

Many teachers differentiate, individualize, and personalize the curriculum for their students because it works best, inspires more learning, and meets every student where they are as it simultaneously helps them move forward.

Should we? Can we differentiate, individualize, and personalize professional development for teachers and other staff?

Should we? Can we instill and model a growth mindset for all educators?

Can we reduce or eliminate one-size-fits-all learning?

Can we honor the expertise, experiences, and knowledge of the teachers in our buildings and meet them where they are so we can help each teacher move forward?

Doesn't everybody moving forward from where they are make more sense than imposing arbitrary standards that few will strive to achieve anyway?

Wouldn't asking the experts in our buildings to share what they know celebrate their experiences, their risk-taking, and their value to our districts while also providing opportunities for leadership?

Shouldn't we champion the work of *Drive* author Daniel Pink and hold autonomy, mastery, and purpose in the highest regard?

Six Unifying Factors for Good Professional Development

It seems that there are at least six unifying factors that should be considered when planning for useful, engaging, robust professional development. The acronym is CHOICE.

1. Constant Progress (C)

We've heard great descriptions of where educators are in their learning. Innovation and educational technology offer a wide range of descriptors: *early-adopter, pioneer, settler, cutting-edge, bleeding-edge, guru, ninja, pirate.* Or *not tech-savvy, tech-averse, just-got-a-smartphone.*

Wherever an individual starts, forward movement is key. Again, we aren't talking about where teachers *should* be. We are talking about where they *are*, and then helping them move forward. Movement is necessary. While everybody starts at a different point, we want each to make progress. By giving teachers the autonomy, opportunities for mastery, and the creation of their own purpose for doing the learning, we will see an inspired movement toward individualized goals. Perhaps one of the goals will also be to move beyond the individualized mindset to a mindset of personalization (where teachers are not only identifying what they need, but also seeking to find the answers on their own).

The bottom line is that they can't end up where they started. Stagnation is not an option; movement is necessary. And when they have learned what they set out to know, they will set new goals. Constant progress.

In our classrooms we would call this a growth mindset. In our professional development we should strive for the same thought process. We don't know now what we want to know, but we are fully capable of identifying what we need and working toward an understanding of it. We can grow and learn just like our students. Indeed, we should be the models for continuous learning and consistent movement forward. What great examples we'll have for our students when we can talk about the time we didn't know something, but struggled through the process of learning about it. Just like we are asking them to do.

And by the way, this progress is for everyone. We can't just count on the younger teachers and administrators to innovate and use technology. In many cases, we need the seasoned veterans to take their vast knowledge and experiences, and connect them with new technologies to assess what will work best. We can't always expect those who are new to the content to also add innovative strategies of the teaching of it. In addition, I don't buy into the idea that younger teachers are "digital natives" and therefore know how to integrate and infuse technology or other innovative approaches. They seem to be more like digital tourists. They use the fun stuff, and enjoy the moment, but they don't live here. They stay up late playing, but then they go home. They aren't using the technology for learning, educating, and connecting.

On a continuum of EdTech use, I see the highest use when students are in middle school. In high school, it is hit-or-miss based on what their teachers are comfortable with. In college they regress even more, it seems, in their use of the latest educational technology. And the low point on the continuum seems to be in schools of education. You are right in thinking that I don't have a peer-reviewed academic study to support this claim, and clearly many programs are doing a phenomenal job preparing their future teachers. Even so, it is a consistent comment from the numerous student teachers I've worked with, talked to, and presented to. Those about to enter the profession would like a little less Piaget and a little more Pinterest.

One recent example came when I presented to a group of about thirty undergraduate students who were preparing to do their student teaching the following semester. I had heard they weren't too tech savvy, so I decided to start talking about something they would be familiar with. When I asked how many were on Twitter, two hands went up. "But not for education," they said. I scrapped some of the other parts of the presentation so I could introduce these students to Twitter and meet them where they were. They moved forward that day and left understanding the power of personalized learning.

2. Honoring Professionals (H)
These people know what they are doing. It's why they were hired, and why they are still here. They probably know what they need next. If we approach every professional development opportunity while repeating those three sentences, it will go a long way.

I was in a planning meeting in a district as they prepared for an upcoming PD day. The plan was to have the teachers choose their session topics, and then have their name tags coded with different colored dots so that we knew where they were supposed to be. The rationale was that the teachers would never remember where they were supposed to be, and more importantly if we didn't have the dots, teachers would go to sessions they didn't sign up for. They'd be bouncing around all over the place instead of where they were "supposed to be." I asked what was wrong with that scenario, and indicated that it sounded a lot like an EdCamp philosophy, where educators vote with their feet. If they aren't getting what they need, they move on (please see page 25 for more on EdCamps).

Let's start the thought-process of PD with those three sentences in our minds. Respect people for what they've done and who they are. Expect that these fine educators will make good decisions in the beginning and be inspired to make great decisions in the future, in large part because we champion their enduring professionalism.

We should probably be asking all of our teachers, and a few individually, if they would share their knowledge. Their peers will want to hear from the practicing teachers in their buildings, and will get to look through the windows into a classroom where innovation is happening. It is a great leadership opportunity for those who accept the invitation. Even if they don't accept the invitation, it's a great way for us to communicate the truth that they have something to contribute. We value what they bring to the table.

What if we went a step further and envisioned educators in our district as movie stars or famous musicians? How would we provide professional learning opportunities for them? Sit them in a big room and show them all the same PowerPoint with remarkably small font? Probably we would recognize, share, and honor what they have already done. We would celebrate their excellence. We would ask them what they want to work on. We would encourage them to show and share what they already know. And we'd probably give them a pretty fancy dressing room with some cool free stuff and drinks. But let's start small and build from there. The educators in our districts *are* celebrities, and we should treat them with the same immutable deference every day.

3. Ongoing (O)
There are times when a brain-dump professional development session or conference can be useful. But we usually need more. We need time to Apply, Practice, and Explore. I call it *Going APE!*.

Educators need the time to take the best ideas and figure out how those could be infused into their curriculum with their students. They need to figure out how to tweak, adjust, and make the idea their own. Educators need the support to implement the ideas, reflect on them, ask more questions, and try the technique or method again. They need someone to bounce ideas off. This could be a formal meeting, a quick email exchange, or an impromptu chat in the hallway to discuss a few questions. It has been my experience that usually teachers need to try an EdTech tool at least three times before they are comfortable enough with it to accurately assess its usefulness. We need to support that process.

The way they do a PLAYDATE would be a fascinating way to do professional development in a district (please see page 67 for more on PLAYDATE). Teachers and administrators would cherish a day to try out the tools, create something for their classes, figure out the best option for their students, and collaborate with colleagues to enjoy the experience of learning more.

And while I don't use the terminology of "play," I understand the concept behind it (and PLAYDATE is a great acronym). To be clear, though, what those outside education may tag as "play," we as professional educators know to be work. I'm learning for my job. I'm exploring. I'm working. When the research scientist is testing new ideas, she usually says she's exploring new theories, and trying to expand on existing research. Similarly, I'm exploring and thinking expansively about the new levels of awesome that can be achieved with our students. This is serious work, my friend.

To facilitate the ongoing process of learning, whether it is in a large group, small group, or individual setting, we should try our best to help everyone get what they need when they need it. It never stops. As educators it should be antithetical to us that we have learning happen in a silo, at a site, on a given day only. We know that learning is constant, progressive, and cumulative. We should model that. We can do it by following up with those individuals we introduced something to. A simple email asking how their implementation is going would be a good start. Short meetings to share progress if progress has been made might be warranted. Even in the large group presentations that I do at conferences, I give my Twitter handle and always tell the participants that they get me for life. Let's keep learning together!

What if we tried to follow the IFF process? Introduce. Facilitate. Follow-up. (I) Here's what you said you need. (F) Let me help you implement it. (F) How's it going? Is it working? What's next?

4. Individualized (I)

Wherever teachers start, the process should honor it. If that teacher needs guidance on why using a Google add-on might be a better process in her classroom, we should help with that. If that teacher needs to know where to locate his computer's mouse, we should help with that. If that teacher wants some ideas on how she could use an educational technology tool to add to a lesson that she already teaches, we should help with that. Whatever they need, we are there for them. The process of Flipped PD seeks to find out where teachers are instead of disregarding it. It asks where you want to go instead of telling you where you should be. We start by asking, "Where are you? Where do you want to go?" The process says it's OK to be you, and we'll help you become an even better version of that. It champions individual needs instead of broadcasting to the large group.

We also recognize that individuals may not know what they don't know. It's acceptable for teachers to ask for a brief overview of several innovative ideas as a way to start the conversation. From there, each teacher can gravitate toward what he or she needs and knows will work best for his or her students.

When we ask educators what they need, and then try to help them get it, we are working to create an Individualized Learning Plan for each educator (please see pages 59 for more information on ILPs). There are some accountability measures here where we are again asking for constant progress. We don't know where each individual will end up. We know where they won't end up: stagnant.

This is hopefully the opposite of a standardized plan for all teachers. We cannot, and should not, paint our whole staff with broad brush strokes. How can you argue with the individualized plan of the teacher who knows what she and her students need? Giving teachers the option to individualize their learning also gives them the incentive to think deeply and expansively about what they could add to their course. I've seen teachers reflect on what they need because they were given the license to innovate. The AP Language teacher decided to create a website so she could curate content for her students. The health teacher just needed her SMART Board realigned, and a way to shorten the URL she needed to share. The science teacher heard about using Google forms for quizzes and wanted to try that along with the Flubaroo add-on to give immediate feedback. The foods teacher wanted her students to set up blogs so they could organize and write about the pictures of the creations they were already sending to instagram on their own. The AP Calculus teacher wanted to create 3D models to help students visualize the problems his students found in their textbook. Even though this is individualized, it is all legitimate, useful learning. And you get a sense that if this were happening in a building, or a district it would be a place of progress and positive movement for students and teacher. Let's provide support and guidance for this process. Instead of engaging in the counterproductive work of forcing a standard or pushing a benchmark on everyone at the same time, let's encourage teachers to identify what they and their students need and then let's help them get it. One piece at a time. One teacher at a time.

5. Collaborative (C)
There should be opportunities for collaboration and sharing ideas, lessons, and applications. These can come in the form of teacher-led presentations and workshops. But they can also come in the form of individuals sharing their progress in small groups. It could be one-on-one conversations with colleagues. Educators have a lot to say and a lot to share. We should not only allow that but encourage it. We may not always have the time or the ability to make this happen, but when we can, we should lean toward a real opportunity for educators to work together on the things they need most. This doesn't mean that every staff meeting should have butcher paper and post-it notes, or that every PD opportunity needs a gallery walk. It means that when authentic opportunities to collaborate present themselves, we should allow them to happen. For example, several of my colleagues noticed that there were constant troubles associated with using the new Google Classroom in our district. In response, they organized a group to try to identify areas of concern and work together on problem-solving solutions. A great opportunity to work together for a common cause.

We should think about this concept the way Flipped Learning teachers do. What is the best use of face-to-face time? What can only be done in the shared space? If we can put the introductory or perfunctory information in the individual space, and use the time together to share ideas, concern, and solutions, we are taking another step in a positive direction.

6. Energizing (E)

The proof is not in the pudding, or the eating. It's in whether or not I want to go out and make my own. After I'm part of professional development, I want to be energized and ready to go. After the best PD, I feel uplifted, energized, and ready to tackle every challenge that presents itself in my professional life. Not only am I ready, but I *want* to do it. I want to apply what I've learned. I want to go create an amazing lesson. I want to innovate and make something better than it was. I want to do it now! Let's go!

This may show up differently for different educators. A good place to start is to make the PD useful, practical, and individualized. If you want to add in a little bit of inspiration, expansive thinking, and fun with a purpose, that usually won't hurt.

In a small group or one-on-one setting, it's easier to individualize. After each experience, we want the learner to say, *Thanks, that's exactly what I needed!* We want them to feel like they got something out of the experience that was useful for them. This was time well-spent. We want them to feel like there is a practical application for their students, and they could implement their new learning tomorrow.

In the smaller setting, it is more challenging to energize through inspiration. It's harder to sprinkle pearls of wisdom, famous quotes, and interesting images from afar when your audience is sitting next to you at the same table. Even so, after discussing very practical ideas, and those ideas that could solve problems in the individual's classroom, I like to include a delicate challenge. "I was thinking that you could also try..." is a good way start. "Now, I was just thinking, what if you thought about trying something like this in the future? Take a look at..." We can encourage expansive thinking even one-on-one.

I shared several useful tools to manipulate population numbers and other geographic data with a geography teacher. Toward the end of our conversation, I suggested "Mystery Skype" where students in different locations interact with each other via Skype or Google Hangout and try to determine where each is located in the world by asking a series of questions. I suggested he could use this as a way of getting his students to think about creating good questions, doing good research, and engaging in metacognition. Our conversation wasn't about data or maps any more. It was about good teaching, good question techniques, and about learning how to learn. We discussed how the power of the "Mystery Skype" was in the question-creation that happens before the online interaction, and in the reflecting, processing, and writing that happens after the interaction is over. Expansive thinking and an energized teacher resulted. He said, "That's a good idea. I think I might try that. Thanks!"

In a large group setting, individualization is more of a challenge. When I present to large groups at a conference or a professional development day, I try to include something for everybody while not lingering on one topic for too long. Options, ideas, examples. What can you take from me, tweak, and use in your own classroom? The best educators are the best thieves (although even the best thieves have to make the loot their own before it has value).

I've toyed with the idea of going more in-depth on one process or one tool and telling multiple stories on one topic. That doesn't seem to be the best option. What if I talk about one tool for fifteen minutes and many in the large group either can't or don't want to use it? I've lost them for fifteen minutes. They aren't energized. They are doing something else, and I may have lost them for the rest of our time together. I think the analogy I used when I spoke at the AP National Conference was appropriate. Since we were in Las Vegas, I offered the participants an extensive buffet where they could choose what they most wanted to add to their plate. Pass some things by and come back for seconds on others. Everyone could get what they wanted. And more.

It's easier to add inspiration, expansive thinking, and fun to the larger group setting, but is still important to do it. Dave Burgess, author of *Teach Like a Pirate*, is my favorite for this type of engagement. Probably because he's the best at it. He is 100% energy combined with audience participation, and magic (not rhetorically...*real* magic). He has an ability to get the audience to think outside of the box. Through his words and his actions, he inspires the audience to think about how they could immediately add what he's sharing to their classrooms and their teaching practices. He is who every teacher and every keynote speaker wants to be (although I don't think I could wear an earring).

Adam Bellow shares a generous helping of images that are sometimes humorous, and serve the purpose of making the audience think how the words could relate to their academic setting. Yong Zhao combines humor and a rich personal narrative to encourage educators to think about the end result of what they do, and plan accordingly. Joe Sanfellippo intensely and enthusiastically entreats his audience to share their district's story, tells how he does it, and then throws stuff at the audience with his #gocrickets hashtag emblazoned on it.

Mostly, we should give educators what they need so that when it's over they don't feel debilitated and beat down. We want them to feel energized, motivated, and inspired. And to tell people about it. In CHOICE, the "E" is *not* silent.

As an example, our school's technology integrator had an hour to share Google apps that teachers might find interesting. Based on what the people in the room needed, the session moved seamlessly back and forth from a presentation to a question-and-answer session, to a workshop, to a collaborative effort with everyone helping each other. During the session one active participant smiled broadly and shared what the full classroom of teachers was thinking: "I feel really good about this whole session." Energized.

Working Toward Other Solutions
In addition to changing our mindset and approaching each professional development experience with the six principles above, we have other practical options as well. For example, in my district I proposed the additional position of Integration Innovator. Through the work and foresight of our Superintendent Kelly Thompson and our CIO Tony Spence, they were able to create this additional position for me. It's like a tech integrator, but it goes well beyond

that. It can be anything from technical instruction on how the SMART Board works, to a discussion of *Teach Like a Pirate*. The whole position is a work in progress and has further iterations that I'm looking forward to implementing.

The plan was that I would start introducing the concept to the whole staff at our school, and they could contact me for what they needed. That has worked well as a starting point. From there I have approached individuals who I think want or need someone to help, suggest, and bounce ideas around with them. I listen at meetings and larger professional development sessions for the questions that teachers and administrators ask, and then I follow up to see if they want to get together and work on creating solutions to their problems. I haven't had anybody turn me down. The next steps will be to contact those who haven't indicated an interest in particular subjects (like cold calls). When we are able to expand the role to more than one hour per day, I'll be able to create an Individualized Learning Plan (ILP) for each teacher, meet with more of them, and help create collaborative groups where they can eventually work together to identify problems and create solutions together. In the future, the group may not need me, or the individual may not need me or the group. It will truly be a pathway to personalized learning. And then they'll blog and tweet about it!

I do want to mention that in the beginning, I got a lot of emails and calls about needing help fixing something related to technology. Questions about how to upload something in Google Drive or how to configure a SMART Board. While this was arguably beyond the scope of this position, I saw it as an opportunity. I could have said, "that's not innovation," or "that's not my job," but I saw this as an opportunity to get in the door and build a relationship. "You need me to add paper to your printer? Sure, I can do that, and let's also talk about how we can use less paper by using Doctopus to share Google Documents with our students." Bam, I'm in!

Indeed, it turns out that those individuals I helped have become the people who have come back to me time and again to innovate and collaborate on other topics for their classrooms. With the two teachers who I helped configure their SMART Board in their new classroom, I've been invited back to help them develop a website and use scheduling apps for in-person meetings with students. With the guidance counselors, whom I helped set up a Twitter account, I've been back several times to talk about how they can use the tool to communicate with students and families about college deadlines, financial aid, presentations they give, and resources that are available. An innovative approach to sharing what they do.

Create a Blog to Share Information
So that others can benefit from the learning that their colleagues are doing, I created a blog to share the activities and examples that we are creating along the way. When one teacher asks about using comic strips to show learning, for example, I blog about it so it can be shared with others. I got a question about this topic one day between classes. And although I couldn't go to that teacher's room at that moment and show her how to implement the ideas, I was able to copy and paste a link to what another teacher had done so she could try to figure it out on her own. While students were coming into my classroom, I was quickly sharing the link with her and was able to still chat with my students between classes as we got ready for another hour of learning. Of course, I always follow up with that teacher to make sure she was able to figure it out, and offer more help on that or the next innovative thing she wants to do. I'm always asking, "What's next?"

Educational technology has been a focus of the innovation that teachers and administrators want to talk about, but there is more. I've been able to discuss teaching strategies and additional innovative ideas to what teachers already do. For one class, we talked about reading and analyzing the Declaration of Independence as a break-up note with American Literature classes. We've talked about giving students an inquiry-based approach where they get several images as clues, and the students have to work collaboratively to make connections by doing research, writing their findings, and making good arguments to support the connections. (This idea came from a conversation at FlipCon with Phil Stubbs @flipyrthinking. He does great work in his classroom, and with using the Verso app.)

Teach Like a Pirate Book Discussion
In addition, we've started a book discussion on the best-selling book *Teach Like a Pirate* by Dave Burgess. We've talked about his innovative ideas and how we could implement them in our

classrooms. Those who show up for the discussions are there on a voluntary basis. We got them a book, and they can choose to read and use whatever parts of it they want to, or they can just show up for a great conversation about great teaching. In a building where there has never really been a book study before, I had to keep adding more people to the group (and ordering more copies of the book). I'm convinced this happened because it wasn't mandatory, and we made it clear that it was about the discussion of better teaching. It wasn't about shoving a method or technique in your face that you didn't want. It was about respecting the professional educator to determine what he or she needed and wanted. We were giving another opportunity to share ideas with colleagues and discuss how to do our work better. We gave the opportunity, and they showed up.

Have A Great Bidet!
Sometimes people won't show up, and we have to accept that. Sometimes we have to find them anyway. As a fun, tongue-in-cheek way to find everybody, I started posting short, useful, edtech ideas in the staff bathrooms. The headline of each says, "It's been hiding, so it's time to Flush Out The Info." The information is printed and taped at eye-level. I call it our version of "sit-and-get." Each in"stall"ment is taped there for about a week, and then is replaced with something new. Usually the template/background is related to the time of year, or a something that is already happening around us (e.g. the week of Veteran's Day, the background included an American flag. For the week of Thanksgiving, we instructed how to manage your "cornucopia of bookmarks.")

Patio PD / Fireside PD
As we considered what other options existed for us to help teachers and administrators to get the learning they wanted and needed, we considered how we could do it closer to home in an atmosphere that was conducive to both learning and comfort. We determined that professional development on our patio could make that happen, and we created PatioPD. Below is how we described it on our website at bretzmanngroup.com:

This is not your usual Professional Development, but it should be. It's on my patio (and maybe yours).

Principles of PatioPD:
1. We like learning together.
2. We like our families.
3. Breaking bread and camaraderie enhance creativity.
4. Informal, personalized, low-stress professional development is useful, powerful, and energizing.
5. Let's get together on my patio to make this happen (e-mail me for the address jbretzmann AT bretzmanngroup.com).

The Setup:
- We will schedule at least five in-person patio sessions that participants can choose from (sessions are 9-Noon, 3-6pm, or 5-8pm). Additional and impromptu sessions could happen upon request.
- Participants for graduate credit will be required to show up for at least three of the sessions. Everybody else is welcome at any time for any amount of time.
- Participants for graduate credit will choose from one of three strands 1. Creating & Designing the Flipped Classroom 2. Flipping 2.0: The Next Steps, or 3. Technology Use to Engage Every Learner and indicate "PatioPD" in the promotional code of the Registration Form (for clerical purposes).
- Participants will learn what they need within their strand with Jason Bretzmann, Kenny Bosch, and/or other experts as their guides.
- Participants for graduate credit will create a blog or micro-blog account (e.g. Twitter) to share what they learn, reflect, and connect to learn more with others
- 3 Graduate Credits come from fully-accredited Calumet College in Indiana
- Bringing families and sharing meals will be encouraged as they will allow for more participation and create a more collaborative atmosphere (kids playing, adults learning, grill ready when you need it).
- Live tweeting will be optional at #patioPD
- Other ideas will be added, subtracted, or enhanced as better ideas emerge

We had several teachers for each session. We explored what they were interested in. We shared ideas, and those who were there worked collaboratively to expand on even more ideas. Teachers enjoyed the process and the outcome so much that they asked if we could do it again *before* next summer. So we created FiresidePD. It's the same principles, but it is in my living room during the Wisconsin winter. This time we've also invited local superstars in education to join the conversation (like the French salons of the late 17th century). We had wonderful learning sessions near my fireplace in January and February. (Note: all wood that we burned was rescued from the local recycle center). Join us! More information at bit.ly/patiopd.

"I Want To Learn This Way For My Professional Development!!"
Whether it is in your living room, on your patio, in a teacher's classroom, or on district professional development days, we have options to flip the mindset of what professional development is, and challenge ourselves to make it something that we want it to be. We have the technology tools available to make the individualized and personalized learning that educators desire become a reality. In the chapters that follow I hope, like I did, that you will write on them that this is the way you want to learn, and that you will also help to make it happen. It takes each of us to begin the process, and start the progression toward more CHOICE in professional development. It may be challenging at first, and we may find some bumps on the pathway to successes, but we have to begin somewhere. The thing about getting started, is that you gotta get started. The rewards you reap from a constantly growing, energized, and thankful staff will be immeasurable.

And let me know how I can help. We are all in this together. From small question, to big keynote, I'm here to help. Let's keep learning together.

Jason Bretzmann is an award-winning social studies teacher, Innovation Integrator, and national speaker. He is co-author and publisher of "Flipping 2.0: Practical Strategies for Flipping Your Class." He also founded and consults with The Bretzmann Group on flipclass, edtech, and personalized PD strategies. Jason has been learning with his students and encouraging innovation since the mid-'90s.

Twitter: @jbretzmann
Email: jbretzmann@bretzmanngroup.com
Website: bretzmanngroup.com Visual Resume: bit.ly/bretzresume

What is Edcamp?

Dr. Kristen Swanson

As we begin to embrace today's shifting definition of "educator," it quickly becomes apparent that we must refocus and re-center our classrooms on the synthesis and creation of content (instead of the mere acquisition of content). For many, this metamorphosis can be exciting and a little bit scary. However, as we mature into digitally sensitive and open educators, we become experts in our own right.

That's where Edcamps come in. Edcamps are free, organic, professional development opportunities by teachers and for teachers. Any educator can hold a session at an Edcamp, and the schedule is determined on the day of the event in response to the most cutting-edge, pressing needs of the group. Based on the concept of open space technology, Edcamp events are derived from the belief that a group of people, given a purpose and freedom, have the ability to self-organize, self-govern, and produce results. Educators who attend Edcamps are treated as experts, and an open exchange of learning and sharing takes place.

Edcamps are...

• **Free:** Edcamps should be free to all attendees. This helps ensure that all different types of teachers and educational stakeholders can attend.

• **Non-commercial and with a vendor-free presence:** Edcamps should be about learning, not selling. Educators should feel free to express their ideas without being swayed or influenced by sales pitches for educational books or technology.

• **Hosted by any organization or anyone:** Anyone should be able to host an Edcamp. School districts, educational stakeholders, and teams of teachers can host Edcamps.

- **Made up of sessions that are determined on the day of the event:** Edcamps should not have pre-scheduled presentations. During the morning of the event, the schedule should be created in conjunction with everyone there. Sessions will be spontaneous, interactive, and responsive to participants' needs.

- **Events where anyone who attends can be a presenter:** Anyone who attends an Edcamp should be eligible to share or facilitate a session. All teachers and educational stakeholders are professionals worthy of sharing their expertise in a collaborative setting.

- **Dependent on "the law of two feet" that encourages participants to find a session that meets their needs:** As anyone can host a session, it is critical that participants are encouraged to actively self-select the best content and sessions. Edcampers should leave sessions that do not meet their needs. This provides a uniquely effective way of "weeding out" sessions that are not based on appropriate research or not delivered in an engaging format.

Edcamp empowers educators and changes the paradigm of professional learning.

Dr. Kristen Swanson has dedicated her entire life to the education profession, and she is incredibly passionate about all aspects of her work. She's served as a teacher, administrator, nonprofit founder, national curriculum authority, and professor. She is currently the Chief of Empowerment for BrightBytes, an Adjunct Professor at DeSales University, and keynote speaker. She is also a founder of the Edcamp Movement.

Personalized PD:
A Teacher's Perspective (Part 2)
Kenny Bosch

When I think about my life experiences in education, I think of all of the teachers that have had an impact on me. From Kindergarten onward, each teacher tried to expose me to new ideas, concepts, and ways to push myself. Along the way these teachers gave me ideas on how to improve upon my strengths and eliminate my weaknesses. I was encouraged by all of these professionals to find ways to personalize my education to help me grow in a way that worked for my needs.

One of the earliest examples of this personalized learning came in first grade with reading groups. We were not put into two or three groups based on ability and speed, but we were given a reading test and then set on a path of growth. Once you mastered the skills of the first reading level, you moved on to the next. I remember feeling proud of myself for advancing to the next stage. I could see improvement, and yet, the work was always a challenge. A great option this reading practice offered was the numerous story choices within each level. I was always able to find stories of interest to me instead of the entire class being required to read the same content.

As I continued on to high school and college, the skills I learned as a maturing person were in place, and I knew which learning styles and study techniques worked best for my learning and growth. When I became a teacher, I thought that this pattern of personal growth in my profession would continue; however, this has not been the case.

When reflecting on professional development from the teacher's perspective, keep in mind the **ABCC**s to help guide administrators' decisions for professional development:

Personalized PD

- A- Attendance
- B- Balance
- C- Choice
- C- Communication

Within each of the concepts above, it is also important to keep these three ideas at the forefront of how professional development should be structured:

1. What is the best use of face time?
2. What content could be flipped to better use face time?
3. How can teachers be involved in the process?
   - Personalize PD to help each teacher grow based on his or her needs.
   - Genuinely incorporate teacher feedback to provide growth for the teacher.

One of my greatest frustrations as an educator has been professional development sessions. I have always viewed myself as a hard-working person, driven to constantly improve. I enjoy learning new information, teaching techniques, and educational technology that I and others may use in the classrooms. I believe that the vast majority of educators are the same type of person: life-long learners. In my fourteen years of experience, I have come across numerous teachers who describe their professional development as one-size-fits-all. This is where the frustration begins.

In my classroom, I have put a high value on face time. We meet with our students for an hour or so a day, and I want to maximize that time focusing on what really matters. I believe that interaction and the sharing of ideas with others is the best use of that face time. When I began my career, I thought that the same value I placed on face time would be cherished when it came to professional development, but I have not found that to be true.

Many teachers would describe a typical professional development meeting by saying that you arrive at PD meetings never really knowing what to expect. Now this may be fine for a first-year teacher or someone new to the district, but if this is the case in every meeting, then change must occur. For many schools, the general practice of setting up a professional development meeting is to email the teachers a few days in advance to inform the staff of the general purpose of the meeting (e.g., reading strategies) and request materials to be brought to the meeting. Upon arrival, we might discuss a topic in which an individual may have limited knowledge; conversely, that individual might discuss a topic they are already using at an advanced level in the classroom. The irritation lies in the pre-conceived idea that the entire staff is at exactly the same point in its learning of the topic, an idea schools do not endorse when it comes to the students we teach.

In our classrooms, teachers are reminded by their administrators to differentiate instruction to best meet the needs of our students. However, when we attend PD, we are not treated in the same fashion. As an example, if you attend PD on the latest technology for use in your classroom, you may be instructed on one tool and all teachers are expected to use that tool. How does this address the varying levels of ability and comfort levels with the technology? Also, if a teacher already uses the technology, is that teacher growing and gaining anything from the meeting? What about a teacher that could not use the technology with their class due to the nature of the students, the type of class, or the learning environment setup?

In the PD environment described above, it is very easy for teachers to become discontented and disinterested. If a teacher already has acquired the skill or technology, there is a natural tendency to tune out the meeting and work towards something else. If a teacher has no background in the skill or technology being taught, he or she may become discouraged and disinterested as well. *Individualized* professional development is the best way to help any staff member grow and take ownership of his or her learning and development.

When the focus of professional development addresses the question, *What is the best use of face time for this teacher?*, then we will see actual professional growth. It may seem basic, but the ideas to consider for developing meetings and teacher/staff involvement are as simple as the **ABCCs**.

The ABCCs of Flipped Professional Development
Attendance
Which staff members actually need to be at this professional development meeting?

We have all been to meetings when we cannot understand why we are in attendance. A teacher I spoke to recently described to me a professional development meeting where the focus was WKCE test scores, analysis of the questions, and methods to improve students' performance. While the teacher could understand her attendance, she could not understand why the custodial staff was also present. She went on to describe her great respect and admiration for the amazing custodial staff that she worked with, but knew the meeting had no value for them or their professional growth.

Likewise, I have been to professional development meetings where the focus was instruction for using a particular technology that I had mastered years ago, while the teacher next to me had never heard of it. In this situation, both of us found little value in the meeting. I already knew the content and how to use it effectively in the classroom, while the teacher next to me was overwhelmed. In my conversations with teachers, many feel that their time is not valued when they must attend a PD meeting regarding how to proctor a given standardized test when their students do not take the test and they are not the ones who will proctor the test. When teachers are required to attend PD meetings that do not benefit their growth, they often feel disappointed by the process and that their time is not valued. The focus of professional development should be on the individual teacher. How can we provide impactful development for each teacher at an individual level and value their face time, or even more simply, time for that matter?

Time is the most precious thing that each of us has. What we do with that time and how we choose to use it, or not use it, has a great impact on each of us. No matter what profession you are in, there is never enough time to get done everything that needs to be done. What makes this reality even more exasperating is being involved in meetings that have no value for you and for which you have no choice to participate. If we can change the format of professional development to encompass choices for the individual that also proves the participants' time is valued, then we have made great progress.

As a teacher, I value my students' time. Each day I have roughly fifty minutes to create a meaningful learning experience for over 140 students. While there can be value in a sit-and-get format, this cannot be the only format used each and every time. As a flipped instructor, I will often use videos to disseminate information that would otherwise take up valuable face time and class work time. By starting with the premise, *What is the best use of face time?*, I am able to make these decisions more easily. As flipped educational ideas are used across the country to benefit students by differentiating instruction, honoring face time, and allowing more student voice and student choice, we have to question why the same opportunities given to our students are denied to those leading them when it comes to their professional development?

Some of the great tools I have used in my own classroom to maximize our face time have allowed me to create videos that I have posted to our Edmodo page. I make these videos at home or at school and alert my students to them to watch prior to our class time. Here are a few examples.

Doceri: This is a whiteboard application that can be used as a stand-alone from your computer or in conjunction with your iPad. My personal preference is to use my iPad when creating videos. Some people like using Doceri because you are not directly in the video; your drawings or documents take center stage. I have used Doceri to make flipped instructions for projects by starting with the rubric for my project on the screen. Then I narrate and draw, highlight, or point out key ideas as I explain the project.

TouchCast: TouchCast.com is a free video creation tool for the iPad. I bought cheap, green fabric from the store and placed the "green screen" onto a tack board in my classroom. I have created flipped parent-teacher conference videos and other content that I send to parents covering basic classroom instruction and format, grading policies, and so on. TouchCast gives you a lot of flexibility in creating your content and is very easy to upload to an email or any website.

In both technology examples above, I began with the premise of *What is the best use of face time?* In my classroom, the best use of class time is getting to work on our projects from the moment my students arrive in the classroom. If a student did not watch the video, they can still watch it before they begin the work. If a student has questions, he or she can ask the questions without keeping the rest of the class from working at its own pace. As for my pre-conference video, the idea is the same. I value the face time I have with parents and do not want to spend it explaining procedural information. Providing this information ahead of time via the video allows me to use the face time during conferences to focus on the growth and potential hurdles for each child as well as learn from parents how to best help their child to grow even further.

While flipped instruction and flipped professional development are great ways to reach our students and staff, you must use the right balance of flipped versus face time. If we keep in mind how to best use our face time, the task of balancing the two becomes easier to handle.

Balance
How much content can be disseminated prior to the meeting to best use face time and yet have staff prepared for the meeting?

As I mentioned earlier, many teachers describe meetings where the expectation for both the focus and learning outcome of the meeting is based solely on the subject listed in the meeting invite. In our classrooms, teachers are instructed to use learning targets to guide student learning. While we don't need learning targets for meetings, we need to know the purpose of the meeting and be prepared to participate.

Whenever I introduce a project in my classroom, I begin by flipping the instructions. I value our face time and flipping the instructions allows us more time to work on the project. Students watch the video (typically 5 minutes or so) the night before class and come ready to begin their work the next day. I begin class by asking a few comprehension questions about the video content as well as asking if there are any questions. If there are none, students begin to work on their projects. If students have questions, they may ask me or a classmate and then begin. Balancing how much information to give in the video versus in the classroom is tricky and takes some practice.

I have made videos before that were too short (a minute or two) and did not provide enough information for my students to come to class the next day (the meeting) and be fully prepared to work. Instead, I had to repeat the material from the video and add more to it during class. In doing so, I used up valuable time. Unfortunately, I have also made videos that were too long and lost my students' interest. My students have told me that videos over five minutes lose their engagement. Based on the feedback from my students, I have focused on balancing the need to cover key ideas while still retaining my students' attention. My students have also told me that they enjoy the video format because if they do not clearly understand some portion of the video they can go back and watch it again. When making videos for flipped professional development, balancing how much information to include with how long to make the video is a key hurdle to successfully cross.

The proper balance of how much content to disseminate prior to a meeting will help staff to feel prepared and ready to learn more at the meeting. If you are in charge of professional development in your building, ask yourself what is the best use of face time? Once you answer that question, you will know what content could be made into a video and then shared with your staff prior to the meeting.

Many teachers are familiar with attending a meeting where they sat and watched a video and were then asked to talk to staff members around them about the video content. I agree with the idea that face time is important and speaking with other colleagues about instruction and best practices is a good idea, but the format of such a meeting could be altered to more effectively use our face time. If the same video is shared with staff a week prior to the meeting, staff members can choose the best time in their schedule to watch the video as well as have enough time to reflect on the ideas covered in the video. This makes each of them more prepared to discuss with others during the meeting. Staff come into the meeting with a clear understanding of what is about to take place instead of finding out as they go. The focus of the meeting changes from taking twenty minutes, for example, to watching a video followed by a short period of time to process and a brief discussion, to having plenty of time in advance to watch and process while leaving forty minutes to discuss during the meeting.

In another example, a professional development meeting is used to review a specific school and school district's test results, and then discuss how test scores could improve. Changing the format of the meeting can make this type of meeting even more effective. In a traditional professional development meeting, an administrator goes over the test scores, explains how a student is placed in a category and explains how the school has placed in the area, county, region and state. While this information is helpful and useful, precious face time is used disseminating data and information that could be covered in a different and more effective format. Alternatively, the test results could be covered by an administrator in a video that is sent to staff prior to the meeting. The staff reflects on its own and researches ways to improve test scores prior to the meeting. The key difference is in the focus of the meeting. It shifts the focus from disseminating data to a staff discussion on ways to improve test scores.

Choice
How can this meeting allow for choice based on interests and abilities?

While flipping professional development is beneficial, we are not going to see true change in professional development unless there is improvement in choices for all staff. When people have a choice they feel empowered to take control and are more likely to find the experience to be a positive one.

The best professional development meeting I have been to was labeled as a learning cafe where teachers had *choices* based on interests and abilities. If you wanted to learn more about SMART boards, you could go to a certain classroom. If you wanted to learn about A.P. test strategies, you could go to a different classroom, and so on. You could feel the energy and excitement in each room as teachers chose which experience would benefit them the most, instead of being subjected to a one-size-fits-all approach. While I felt comfortable with the latest technology, there were staff members still struggling with managing their (then new) Google account. Instead of these late learners of technology feeling shunned, they were empowered to learn more. In any case, the advantage of this learning cafe was the choice that it afforded each and every teacher. Teachers took control of their learning and professional development, and it led to the staff wanting more experiences like this one. Too often, teachers are not given choices in their professional development, which results in missed opportunities to truly help staff to grow further as professionals.

At most meetings and professional development sessions, teachers of different grade levels, content areas, and backgrounds are all sitting through a one-size-fits-all agenda. When these types of meetings occur, the majority of the room is not engaged. In my flipped classroom, student choice is available each and every day. I teach U.S. History and my students are able to choose an area of study to dig deeper and learn more about as it relates to our chapter. For example, if we are studying the early 1800's, students can choose to learn about Thomas Jefferson in any direction they choose: personal life, invention, presidency, etc. Students can choose to go in a completely different direction and learn about hunting practices, foods, clothing styles, and more of the time period. The limitless choices excite my students because they are in control of their learning.

After my students chose a topic, they then make more choices. Do they want to work with a partner or alone? They can work with a partner from the same class period or any other class that I have throughout the day. They have a list of over forty technology options with which to present their learning. If they find a new technology, they may use that as well and add it to our group list. Some of my students do not enjoy using computers, so I have had students present in a format they enjoy. One student turns in drawings of his research, one student sang a song from the time period because she enjoys singing, and others enjoy cooking and have baked food from various time periods. When we add choice to the equation, we will have even greater results. If administrators and school leaders can add choice to professional development, then they will see an increased excitement for and engagement with professional development.

There are multiple ways to individualize professional development:

1. Create Videos
Make informational videos so that staff can come to the meeting ready to participate. Sending videos to staff at least a week prior to a meeting allows staff to choose when viewing the content fits into their schedule. Another option is to send a link of a video of information covered at meetings and allow staff to show up later to a meeting if it is going to be covered at the beginning of a meeting. This way, if staff members want to watch the video with the group at the actual meeting, they still have that option.

2. Provide Multiple Dates
Plan for multiple professional development options throughout the school year and summer, and allow teachers to choose which ones fit their needs. If you want to set a number of professional development meetings that the staff need to attend, then make sure there are numerous options. For example, if six professional development courses are required, perhaps 30 courses can be offered throughout the entire year to give staff the flexibility to choose what works best for their schedule. Allow and encourage attendance at conferences to count towards professional development.

3. Provide Professional Development at Multiple Times
It is essential to be aware of your staff's scheduling needs when it comes to offering professional development. Teachers are often pulled in many directions because of classroom prep needs, extracurricular coaching and advising, students needing before- and after-school help, childcare or aging parent needs, and more. For these reasons, the greater the flexibility for teachers, the more open they will be towards their professional development. Offer professional development before school, during the school day (half days with sub coverage) or after school, as well as throughout the summer.

4. Allow for Teamwork
Encourage, but do not force, staff to work on professional development with a colleague. Allowing staff members to go to conferences with a colleague increases the chances that staff will attend. Be open to the many ways professional development can and is already taking place; realize that some of the best PD is happening

in your own building throughout the day in an informal format when a colleague seeks out another's help or advice. If, as a principal or school leader, you feel you must have proof of professional development, ask your staff members to show you how they have grown professionally during the year from their work with a colleague in some format that they choose.

When considering how to best serve your staff and change professional development into the powerful growth you would like to see, the easiest way to make that happen is to simply ask your staff for their input. If teachers are involved in the decisions impacting their professional development, feel valued and are communicating what their needs are, then teachers will feel empowered and motivated to continue their own professional growth.

Communication
How can the staff communicate with each other and their administrative leaders about what they need next in order to grow?

Any good relationship is based on solid communication. Communication is essential to helping a relationship to grow and only takes place when there is trust between both parties. Both parties have to trust that the other genuinely cares about them and wants to see them happy, they have to be willing to speak the truth even when what you say could be hurtful, and they have to be responsive to each other and make adjustments when necessary.

I am sure each of us can think of a time we were asked what we truthfully thought about someone else's decisions. We may hesitate to give a truthful opinion if we are unsure of its impact to the other person. If you have not established a relationship based on trust, it is that lack of trust that makes us hesitate. In my classroom, I work very hard from day one to establish trust with my students. They know that I care about them, their education and their well-being. After this level of trust is established, true communication can take place.

This past year I taught middle school history for the first time. I thought my students could handle reading at a certain pace as well as take their own notes and complete a technology project within a week. At first the pace was a little difficult for them, but I communicated with them that I knew they could get the work done. I established trust by not grading the first few practice assessments. This helped alleviate fear and allowed them to trust that I cared about their growth. As time went by, I assumed they could handle an even quicker pace. We tried to read more per day for each chapter, and at the end we assessed how it went. My students knew I cared about them and would listen to their opinions. We established a level of trust that allowed us to communicate effectively. I listened to my students, slowed down our pace, and returned to the original format.

While this next example may seem simple, it confirms the impact of trust and communication. I started the school year by asking my students which day of the week they would prefer to have their chapter projects due, and they voted on Fridays. After a few chapters, they communicated openly to me that they would like to have the project due dates moved to Mondays so that they could use the weekend to complete their work. The bottom line for me is that my students take ownership of their work, are adequately prepared, and have an increased level of understanding. As far as which day of the week the project was due made no real difference to me, but mattered greatly to my students. By listening to their concerns and making the adjustment, the students felt more involved in the direction of the class and their learning. More importantly, my students knew that I have a genuine concern and care for them and because of this, they trust that I will listen and be responsive to their needs going forward.

As a teacher, I would like to see more trust established and improved communication when it comes to professional development. I believe that many teachers feel that professional development is created regardless of their individual strengths and areas of growth and that their professional opinions on matters that are important to them are often disregarded. When this feeling exists, it is counterproductive to establishing trust and open communication. The question then is, *How do we flip professional development to better help teachers grow?*

Flipped professional development is different as it starts with valuing your staff and seeing them as valuable assets to your school and community. The focus has to be on establishing trust with your staff so that they can communicate openly, honestly, and professionally with administration about what is working well and what is not. Administrators and school leaders need to be willing to hear both positive and negative feedback as well as be responsive to the needs of their staff.

In my classroom, I have used PollEverywhere.com to gauge where my students' comfort level was with our class pace. After seeing the results, I had a conversation with each class and responded to their needs by making a reasonable adjustment to our pace. The trust level I established with my students by listening to their concerns carried on throughout the year. Later in the year, I used other tools to gauge student comfort levels: Edmodo polls (edmodo.com), Socrative exit tickets (socrative.com), and Google Forms to assess where each class was in the process. As time went on, I established trust in our communication process to such a deep level that I no longer needed these tools and could simply ask my classes, and they would speak their opinions publicly.

Flipped professional development can lead to the same level of trust and communication. I would like to see administrators begin the year by asking staff what each person needs as an individual to grow professionally. When feedback is received, I would like to see those opinions and wants for professional growth to be honored as much as possible. Staff can be surveyed for ideas on professional development at the start of the school year through any of the methods mentioned above, or numerous others. Once a professional development session ends, administrators can again use a tool listed above to gauge what could have been done better and/or what direction needs to be taken next to best serve their staff. When the staff sees that their opinions matter and are welcomed, they will be more willing to give them and see the benefit of professional development.

The term differentiate or differentiation is used to describe how teachers should change instruction to best meet the needs of each student at his or her developmental level. The flipped classroom is the best model to actually make differentiation a reality. My hope is that by using flipped professional development, the same goal of differentiation for each teacher can become a reality as well.

Kenny Bosch *has been an educator and coach since 1999 earning his Master's Degree in Education through the University of Wisconsin – La Crosse as part of their blended education program, and has taught A.P. U.S. History, U.S. History and World History. Since 2012 he has been an educational consultant and has presented at local seminars and workshops. He is co-author of the award-winning book "Flipping 2.0: Practical Strategies for Flipping Your Class." Kenny was named the 2013 "Outstanding Educator" by Lawrence University for his ability to connect with and inspire students. He is a Doceri certified teacher.*

Twitter: @kennybosch
Website: kennybosch.blogspot.com

What is Camtasia?
Brian Bennett

Staff meetings are unavoidable. Administrative information is sometimes state-mandated and sometimes related to student safety At the same time, teachers' and administrators' time is precious. Instructional time is important, and the hours in between classes need to be well-spent to make sure planning and grading are completed.

How can you begin to reclaim time during the day?

Flipped staff meetings are becoming more popular with department heads and administrators across the country. Rather than sending a "wall-of-text" email or calling a meeting to discuss the lunch policy, leaders are creating short videos teachers can watch whenever—and wherever—they have a few free moments. Many times, this information can be given in ten minutes or less. Now, full meetings can be spent on discussion or implementation of the information given. Question-and-answer time isn't relegated to the end of the meeting, but rather *becomes* the meeting.

How is this done?

TechSmith makes easy-to-use, screen capture software that can be used to record anything you see on your computer screen. Teachers have been doing this since the mid-2000's with the growth of Flipped Learning, but it is just beginning to spill over into the administrator's role.

Camtasia is TechSmith's screen recording and editing suite. It gives users the ability not only to record their screens, but also allows them to edit and enhance those videos to promote interaction and engagement from the viewers. We've learned a lot by watching teachers and administrators alike use the software, and we have some tips for anyone just starting out with using video to support staff.

1. **Keep your videos short.** Think about getting a video in your email. What's the first thing you look at? For most people, it's the length of the clip. Remember, we're trying to *save* time here. Your viewers are less likely to open—let alone engage with—a video that is too long. The "sweet spot" we've seen is between five and eight minutes. With no interruptions, you can fit a lot into that timeframe. If your video is longer, consider splitting it up into multiple parts.

2. **One idea per video**. This helps accomplish the first goal. By limiting the amount of information in each video, you're helping your viewers both take in and digest the information. In other words, don't overload! If you have multiple topics to cover, consider a short video series of clips rather than one long video.

3. **Use callouts to draw attention.** Unlike sitting in a meeting, you do not have control over where your audience looks. Consider using a callout (text bubble) to draw the viewer's attention to your main idea. It can be as simple as an arrow on the screen to point to a PowerPoint bullet.

4. **Use your existing notes.** Your videos do *not* have to be Hollywood productions to be effective. If you already have a PowerPoint with notes for the meeting, you're all set to record your video. Talk through your slides like you would in the meeting and share it out.

5. **Reimagine your meeting time.** Now that your video is done and shared, you need to rethink your meeting time. Don't go over the same information with the whole group! What would you *like* to do with the extra time? Now is your chance to change staff meetings to an interactive format rather than sit-and-get.

6. **Take feedback.** Make sure you solicit feedback from your staff about the efficacy of the video. What did they like? What didn't they like? By getting feedback on your use of video for information distribution, you'll ensure that when you send it out, people will watch it. You'll also improve as a communicator, and the process will support itself.

This is not an overnight shift. There may be some training involved with getting teachers to watch instructional content. Consider sending along the questions you'll be using in the meeting to spur discussion or debate. Give teachers an expectation of what they should get by watching the video. In other words, think about what you would do as a teacher asking students to watch a video for homework. The situations are similar, and using those principles from the classroom will help you get off on the right foot.

Brian E. Bennett is a former and current Chemistry teacher with experience in a variety of educational settings. He was the Academic Solutions Engineer at TechSmith, a software company in Okemos, MI before he headed back to the classroom. He is co-author of Flipping 2.0: Practical Strategies for Flipping Your Class *and a frequent conference speaker on the best methods for teaching and learning. When Brian isn't working, he likes to write on his blog, dabble with new ideas, and read.*

Twitter: @bennettscience
Website: ohheybrian.com

Flipped Professional Development Through Coaching
Kristin Daniels

The education field is facing dramatic changes. In a system that has changed its process very little, we are facing disruptive innovations from technologies that are changing how we define education. Professional development is necessary for schools and districts to close the technology adoption gap and move *all* teachers towards implementing innovative ideas in their classrooms. Effective professional development is personalized, job-embedded, and technology-infused.

Challenges with Traditional PD
When thinking about innovative ways to deliver professional development, you need to evaluate what works and what doesn't work in your existing model. Let's consider "traditional PD", typically a one-time gathering of educators to learn about one particular tool, process, or strategy. Just like a traditional classroom, traditional PD approaches learning as a one-size-fits-all model. The challenges of this setting is that content delivery is at one pace, one style, one time, and there is no follow-up with the participants. Teachers bring a variety of experiences, skills, and interest levels to the group. An instructor will adjust as much as possible to meet the needs of all participants. But as any teacher knows, it is challenging to meet the needs of everyone in this type of setting. We know that this is not the best way to learn.

Another challenge to traditional PD is that teachers are provided very little time for their own learning. For students, the traditional learning cycle typically includes direct instruction, guided practice, independent practice, and assessment. Traditional teacher professional development provided by a school or district usually includes direct instruction and perhaps some guided practice. There is rarely follow up. It is a typical sit-and-get situation.

While there are many reasons for eliminating this type of top-down professional development altogether, many schools and districts only have the capacity for "one-time" professional development. Creating a professional development model that provides ongoing support for teachers to move towards a school's or district's long-range vision demands a team of individuals who work year-round to create such a program. Recently, more and more schools are combining their teaching and learning department with the technology department to create a partnership between two vital components of a school district. This collaboration creates a thorough approach to curriculum, instruction, and the technology that inevitably will be used in each learning environment. Significant and sustainable teacher development requires a team of coaches to work with teachers; coaches that are well-versed in instruction and technology integration. Information today, and for our foreseeable future, is easily accessible. Today's learners, young and not-so-young, require a facilitator or coach to help them explore content at a deeper level.

Why Flipped Professional Development

If you consider what many call "flipped classroom 101", we know that there is much information that we can provide students before meeting with them face-to-face, and much can be gained by this preparation. However, as a teacher extends themselves past a "flipped classroom 101" mentality and towards supporting a learning cycle that allows students to move at their own pace and to access content when they need it, the impact on student learning increases. This continuum from *differentiation* to *individualization* and all the way to *personalization* can also be applied to professional development. This movement is best seen in various implementations of professional learning, from creating flipped faculty meetings and flipped professional development days all the way to the more personalized flipped professional coaching.

It is important to create, curate, and organize digital content for teachers. However, simply providing digital content for teachers and calling it "flipped professional development" would be the same as providing video lessons to students and calling it a "flipped classroom." Flipped Learning is about more than the videos. It is about the change that takes place during the face-to-face time. Flipped Learning happens when a teacher creates an environment that allows learners to explore content at a higher level, using higher-order thinking skills like "compare", "create", and "design", instead of lower-order thinking skills like "recall", "summarize", or "describe". Flipped Learning teachers use digital content with *intention*, sharing specific content with learners in their individual learning space and at the appropriate time in their learning cycle. This is why the video is important.

Flipped Professional Development Variations
Currently, a number of flipped professional development models have emerged since Flipped Learning moved into the school environment. Each of the variations was created to enhance an existing professional development setting. Flipped faculty meetings provide an easy entry point into flipped learning while flipped workshops can provide teachers the opportunity to explore a topic in greater depth. Ultimately, flipped professional coaching has the greatest impact on teachers. But like a flipped classroom, flipped professional development models require many iterations to meet the needs of individuals, schools, and districts. If teachers want to change how time is spent with students, they must first begin by changing the way they spend time with colleagues. One of the easiest starting points for exploring flipped learning is to begin thinking about ways you can improve your own learning opportunities.

Flipped Faculty Meetings and Flipped Workshops
Consider faculty meetings, whether they are once a month or once a week. Coming together as a school staff should be positive; a time for collaborating, sharing, and celebrating. Teachers should look forward to these meetings and should leave each meeting feeling energized and enthusiastic about the students, their colleagues, and the school community. Could monthly faculty meetings look similar to a meeting of camp counselors just before the campers arrive? Can you imagine a meeting packed with energy, enthusiasm, and anticipation? Faculty meetings have traditionally been a time to deliver content. At best, leaders ask staff to follow-up in grade level groups or plan for follow-up with everyone at the next meeting. At worst, educators are expected to implement something to which they were just introduced. Moving back into their classroom and into

their daily routine leads to resentment for an ever growing list of things to tackle in isolation. Traditional faculty meetings perpetuate the idea that teachers work in isolation. Faculty meetings are "flipped" when important information is accessed before the meeting and consequently changes how colleagues spend their time together. The resulting meeting generates energy and momentum throughout the organization.

During a (typical) traditional professional development workshop, the instructor begins by introducing themselves and the topic that they will be talking about. The instructor is clear and concise, sharing information and answering questions about the topic along the way. Some participants are new to the topic, some are familiar, and some may not see how it relates to their classroom. The face-to-face time is precious. It is necessary for the instructor to get participants excited and connected with the topic within this time frame. Ideas are presented in creative and impressive ways, showcasing the topic to participants. Teachers are jazzed.

Keep in mind the challenges of traditional professional development already mentioned. What are the outcomes of this type of traditional learning environment? For some, it works just fine. However, to reach all individuals, the challenges of this learning environment need to be minimized, if not removed altogether.

Re-imagine this time. There are two parts. There is the face-to-face time that is precious and sacred. This time should be spent doing things that we cannot do alone. And there is the "flipped" part of this meeting or workshop. What can we do to prepare for this time together? How can we get ourselves ready to maximize our limited time together?

Plan for face-to-face time. This comes first. There are many reasons why you gather in a group. A typical meeting (faculty or workshop) uses face-to-face time for sharing information. But the real value of face-to-face time is that by being together you have the opportunity to *exchange* (this means two ways) ideas and information, rather than just receive information. Even better, you generate *new* ideas and innovations that would not have be created otherwise. Examine your current meeting structure. Is it necessary to gather together for the items on your agenda? Or could many of these items be shifted into the individual learning space. Can the purpose for gathering together be something more meaningful?

As you plan for this time, continue to ask: *What's the benefit of being together?* And, for now, don't be anxious if you're not sure where to start. Select topics that are relevant to the teachers. Because face-to-face time will not be used for disseminating information, you can have more than one topic being discussed at the meeting. Review helpful team-building, decision-making and group-facilitation strategies. Slowly add activities that allow teachers to engage with one another and explore content at a deeper level.

Face-to-face meetings could give staff the time, space and resources to:

- Work in grade-level teams to explore specific instructional strategies
- Participate in a whole-group, team-building activity
- Share innovative projects happening throughout the school
- Discuss school issues and policies as a whole group
- Work in cross-curricular groups to discuss student-centered pedagogy
- Brainstorm ideas for improving classroom space
- Share strategies for shifting the learning culture of the classroom
- Discuss best practices for formative and summative assessment
- Engage in discussion about classroom management
- Organize their own "unconference"

Get teachers excited by letting them PLAY! This time is perfect for modeling new technology tools or classroom strategies with teachers. Let the teachers be engaged in the process, allowing them to experience a student's perspective and then reflect with colleagues. It's important for our teachers to constantly be engaged in professional conversation about the classroom and, ultimately, the students.

Don't forget to capture this time together by snapping a few photos or capturing a few minutes of video. Instant upload of the images and video from a mobile device to an online storage site makes sharing these moments at a later time extremely simple.

Prepare materials ahead of time. The next step is to consider how you could support your face-to-face plans. Think of these three strategies as you build materials for teachers: SHARE - GATHER - CONNECT. What will staff need to do so they are prepared to spend their time efficiently and engaged in the process? How can you connect your staff with one another before the meeting begins? Here are some common ways to flip your staff learning. Choose one strategy, combine two, or use all three for preparing "flipped" materials.

Share
Provide access to the meeting agenda using Google Docs. To go one step further: Allow staff to create the agenda and edit items, if necessary. Providing access to the agenda increases transparency among staff; transparency increases trust. Provide links to any resources that will be discussed or referenced during a meeting. By doing this, you will be able to explore content at a deeper level.

Tip: Consider the way that information is communicated to staff. Is there a consistent process? Is information archived in a way that makes it easy to retrieve? Do teachers know what is available and where to find it? Go to flippedpd.org/share for an updated list of various tools that can be used to share information with staff before a meeting.

Gather
Conduct a survey to collect information prior to the meeting. Use the information to create working groups, spur discussion, or determine face-to-face plans. Sometimes meetings will include a brief showcase of instructional strategies or technology tools. Surveys can be helpful in revealing information about staff interest or questions regarding this content. Immediately sharing survey results is one way to connect teachers with one another before the meeting begins.

Assess for understanding. If you really want to know what teachers understand about your meeting topic, give them a short assessment using a tool that they might be able to use in their classroom. This modeling is professional development on its own! Teachers will use their experience as a learner to make adjustments to the options they provide for their students. Today, there are many tools and methods for formative assessment. Let your teachers experience this as a student.

Tip: Expand your ideas about surveys. Today, there are easy-to-use tools that allow you to collect feedback from your staff in a variety of ways (text, audio, or video). How will this change what you want to ask your staff? Go to flippedpd.org for updated suggestions on useful tools for gathering information as well as unique formative assessment tools.

Connect
Begin the conversation using asynchronous communication tools to engage in meaningful conversation on your own time. Pose a question to your staff, and then give them some time to begin discussion with one another on the given topic. Track their conversation and add information and comments when needed.

Tip: Kick it up a notch during the face-to-face time by providing them with a task to complete based on the topic area. Create a task that is dependent on prior knowledge, knowledge that would have been covered in early conversations online. Go to flippedpd.org/connect for an updated list of online tools that you can use with teachers to begin a discussion before meeting face-to-face.

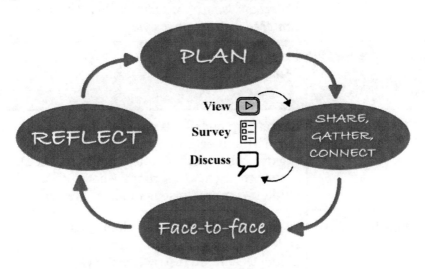

With appropriate digital materials (intentional content) viewed prior to meetings, time can be used to collaborate with colleagues and explore issues at a deeper level.

Flipped Professional Development In Action
Let's take a look at the following example of a Flipped PD plan. The Flipped Strategies/Materials can be used alone or in combination with one another.

Topic: Using Classroom Space to Support Student-Centered Instructional Strategies

Flipped Strategy	Flipped Materials
SHARE	Create a video that shows images of a classroom space before and after a classroom makeover. Highlight how changes made to the classroom space minimize pedagogical challenges and support student-centered instruction.
GATHER	Have participants draw a map of their current classroom configuration and upload to a shared space. If participants want to share pictures, provide a tool and workflow for them to do so.
CONNECT	Allow participants to respond asynchronously to a discussion prompt: *How does your current classroom space support or hinder a student centered instructional style?*
Face-to-Face Meeting Strategy	**Face-to-Face Plan**
ENGAGE	If staff uploaded classroom maps, take time during the meeting to talk about one or two of the maps. Discuss possible changes that could be made to each classroom space to support student-centered instructional strategies.
COLLABORATE	Working in grade level teams, have teachers redesign their classroom space to best support a student-centered instructional style.

Download the preceding Flipped Professional Development worksheet from flippedpd.org

In the example, the face-to-face time becomes collaborative work time to address an existing issue and use collective knowledge to create a plan that will impact student learning. In a flipped faculty meeting or a flipped workshop, the time spent together becomes time for group reflection, collaboration, conversation, discussion, and celebration. Teaching can be a very isolating profession. Do not isolate your teachers during this time. Bring them together. You are building the necessary foundation for creating a community of collaborative learners. Encourage professional discourse and help strengthen their relationships by provided an engaging, meaningful, and respectful learning opportunity for them each month. In addition, this will empower teachers to take their experience and create something similar for their students.

After the face-to-face meeting time, plan to provide a "reflection" on the topic. This could be a summary of your collaborative work on the topic or an opportunity for extended exploration for those who are interested. It is important to provide a "next step" in the learning cycle, whether that is an action item or a plan to follow-up at a later time, so that this does not become a one-time event.

Flipped Professional Coaching
Research has shown that teacher quality affects student achievement. It is imperative that we plan to support the professional, lifelong learning of teachers! Therefore, effective professional development is critical and cannot be undervalued. More than any other professional development model, coaching increases the implementation rates of learned skills into the classroom. Ultimately, the best professional development that you can provide for teachers is through a coaching model.

Coaching is personalized from the start. By embracing the ideas of Flipped Learning and applying them towards professional development, you will be able to use digital content to convey important information and minimize large-group, face-to-face time, making coaching a feasible model. This is a natural progression of flipped learning. For example, in a flipped classroom, as direct instruction is shifted out of the large group space, the teacher naturally moves into more of a coaching role in order to create a more personalized learning environment.

Like any professional development model, flipped professional coaching requires structure. Careful consideration of how you will structure face-to-face time, document teacher progress, and utilize digital content is critical to the success of flipped professional coaching. But most of all, just as the flipped classroom demands that students become more responsible for their own learning, flipped professional coaching requires teachers to embrace self-directed learning. This can be the greatest challenge of all and can be accomplished by establishing trusting relationships and a positive culture of lifelong learning.

Flipped Professional Coaching Learning Cycle
The flipped professional coaching learning cycle has very similar components to other varieties of flipped PD. The first step in this process is for the teacher and coach to meet to that they can explore options, interests, and strengths. Based on this information and any school or district goals, together the teacher and coach will formulate a personal goal for the teacher. From here, it is the job of the coach to provide resources (digital content, time, technology, coaching, etc.) so that the teacher can implement projects or strategies in their classroom in order to meet their goal. Finally, teachers should be encouraged to share their stories. Whether their goal was to create a project for students or increase student achievement in a particular area, they should be encouraged to share what they have learned. This information contributes to the common knowledge of a school or district and can be utilized to move towards shared goals and understanding.

The flipped professional coaching learning cycle

Just as there are many teaching strategies, there are many wonderful coaching frameworks available for schools to implement. Regardless of the framework you decide upon, flipped professional coaching has the advantage of using digital content to share important and customized information with the teacher so that face-to-face time can be used for personalized coaching.

Creating Time for Teachers

Flipped professional coaching requires designated small-group or individual meeting time for teachers and coaches. It is vital to create consistently scheduled face-to-face meetings with teachers so that teachers can begin to ask questions and have conversation that will help them to reflect on their practice and seek ways to improve their teaching. By providing time and space for natural conversation to occur between a teacher and a coach, opportunities reveal themselves. A perceptive coach will navigate these opportunities and work with the teacher to develop a reasonable goal. Scheduled time provides structure and consistency.

Every school will have different opportunities for meeting time. Some common options for one-on-one or small-group time include:

- Non-student time (before school, after school, prep periods, lunch break, summer break)
- Common planning time
- Designated PLC time
- Create time during the day (rotating sub model)

If you choose to create face-to-face time with teachers during the workday, consider a model that uses rotating substitute teachers to relieve groups of teachers throughout the day so that they can meet with coaches each month. Although group size can be adjusted (affecting the number of subs needed on one day), the model remains the same: bring in substitute teachers to work a rotating schedule, relieving teachers one at a time. For a workshop schedule with groups of three teachers meeting throughout the day, a building would hire three all day subs for the day.

Working with teachers in small groups allows for exploration of personal interests.

Grade	First Name	Last Name	Workshop Day	Workshop Time	Flipped PD ILP
Workshop Day 1 (9/24, 10/22, 11/12, 1/14, 2/25, 3/25)					
3			1	8:00 AM	https://docs.google.com/
3			1	8:00 AM	https://docs.google.com/
3			1	8:00 AM	https://docs.google.com/
1			1	10:30 AM	https://sites.google.com/
1			1	10:30 AM	https://docs.google.com/
1			1	10:30 AM	https://docs.google.com/
2			1	1:00 PM	https://docs.google.com/
2			1	1:00 PM	https://docs.google.com/
2			1	1:00 PM	https://docs.google.com/
Workshop Day 2 (9/25, 10/23, 11/13, 1/22, 2/26, 3/26)					
5			2	8:00 AM	https://docs.google.com/
5			2	8:00 AM	https://docs.google.com/
4			2	9:30 AM	https://docs.google.com/
4			2	9:30 AM	https://docs.google.com/
6			2	11:00 AM	https://docs.google.com/
6			2	11:00 AM	https://docs.google.com/
4.5			2	12:30 PM	https://docs.google.com/
4.5			2	12:30 PM	https://docs.google.com/
4.5			2	12:30 PM	https://docs.google.com/
6			2	2:00 PM	https://docs.google.com/
math with me			2	2:00 PM	https://docs.google.com/

Sample flipped professional coaching workshop schedule

This figure above shows an example of a school that has committed to two flipped PD workshop days each month for six months (September, October, November, January, February and March). Teachers are organized into grade-level teams. On Workshop Day 1, teams of three teachers meet with a coach for a two and a half hour block of time. A total of nine teachers are seen on the first day. On Workshop Day 2, the teams of two teachers meet with the coach for an hour and a half. A total of 10 teachers are seen on the second workshop day.

Grade	First Name	Last Name	Workshop Day	Workshop Time	FlippedPD ILP
Workshop Day 1 - 6 subs (10/3, 11/8, 1/10, 3/19)					
0			1	8:00 AM	https://docs.google
0			1	8:00 AM	https://docs.google
0			1	8:00 AM	https://docs.google
2			1	8:00 AM	https://docs.google
2			1	8:00 AM	https://docs.google
2			1	8:00 AM	https://docs.google
1			1	12:00 PM	https://docs.google
1			1	12:00 PM	https://docs.google
1			1	12:00 PM	https://docs.google
1			1	12:00 PM	https://docs.google
5			1	12:00 PM	https://docs.google
5			1	12:00 PM	https://docs.google
Workshop Day 2 - 5 subs (10/10, 11/7, 1/15, 3/20)					
3			2	8:00 AM	https://docs.google
3			2	8:00 AM	https://docs.google
3			2	8:00 AM	https://docs.google
3			2	8:00:00	https://docs.google
2nd			2	8:00 AM	https://docs.google
6			2	12:00 PM	https://docs.google
6			2	12:00 PM	https://docs.google
6			2	12:00 PM	https://docs.google
6			2	12:00 PM	https://docs.google
PE			2	12:00 PM	https://docs.google

Flipped Professional Coaching Workshop Schedule

This figure above shows another example of a school that has committed to two flipped PD workshop days each month for four months (October, November, January, and March). Teachers are primarily organized into grade level teams with a few exceptions. On Workshop Day 1, two teams of three teachers each meet with a coach for a four hour block of time. The second group of teachers is relieved by the rotating subs and begin their session at 12:00 pm. A total of twelve teachers are seen on the first day. Workshop Day 2 is similar to the first day.

Document Workshop Resources and Teacher Learning Goals

In the far right column of the flipped PD schedules above, you will see a link to the teachers' Individual Learning Plans. Using Google Docs, an informal Individual Learning Plan (ILP) was created for teachers participating in flipped PD (find a template at flippedpd.org).

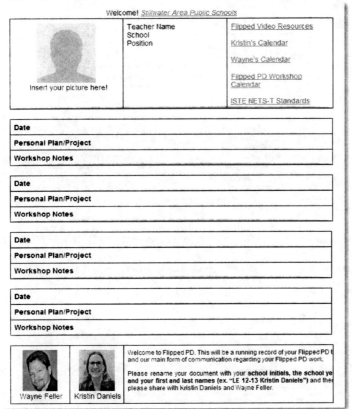

A Google Doc template for an Individual Learning Plan (ILP) used with teachers in Flipped PD.

Once created, teachers can share their ILP with colleagues, coaches and mentors. This document is edited by many and used to record the teacher's personal goals, plans, and projects. Workshop notes are entered, and personalized digital content links are pasted directly into the document for teachers to access at any time. It is important to support teachers throughout their learning cycle by maintaining documentation, providing personalized digital resources, and establishing easy methods for communication. The individual documentation helps hold teachers accountable for the goals that they have set.

Flipped Video Resources
Kristin's Calendar
Wayne's Calendar
Flipped PD Workshop Calendar
ISTE NETS-T Standards

Date 10/3/12

Personal Plan/Project Short term-Conference video for parents, Long term goal-PTA video & website

Workshop Notes - iMotionHD a great app to take a picture every 10 seconds. Put documents on Google Docs. Google Docs video tutorials.

Date 11/812

Personal Plan/Project Short term make a video and send it to a student, Long term- WEB SITE!

Workshop Notes Worked on website, website tutorials

Date 1/10/13

Personal Plan/Project 1. Look at KidsBlog (it's crashing) 2. Refresh my memory on Educreations. 3. Put Photos on website (I couldn't get it to work.) 4. Work on my blog. 5. Newsletter put up.

Workshop Notes
From Kristin - Blogging with kids: Take a look at the idea of "Quadblogging" by reading this blog post by Suzie Boss. When you have more time, you can watch Paul Allison's *Teachers Teaching Teachers* video podcast where he and a number of other educators talk about quadblogging.
Read the posts on Quadblogging. What is our district's policy?

Here is the email lists video
more great nudges ... (global classroom project)

Date 3/19/13

Personal Plan PTA slideshow, fix Kidblog, fix printer problem.

An individual teacher's ILP. Note the separate workshop dates and the linked video tutorials and links in upper right-hand corner.

A Coach's Perspective - Teacher ILPs in Google Drive.

Creating scheduled follow-up gives them the time and support they need to implement new ideas in the classroom. Carefully prepared professional development plays a critical role at each part of the learning cycle in order to maximize personal professional growth for teachers.

The "flip" in Flipped Professional Development
Approaching Video Creation
Video is an engaging way to communicate information. It is becoming extremely easy to create video in order to communicate information, whether the purpose is to provide technical information about technology or to communicate pertinent information before a face-to-face meeting.

Depending on how you approach video creation for professional development, deciding on the tools, workflow, storage, and delivery can be overwhelming. It is much easier to start at a personal level and figure out how you as a professional want to use video in your everyday work. Look at the grassroots work of Flipped Learning educators over the last few years. Most of these pioneers started independently of their colleagues.

Thoughtfulness in the creation and organization of digital content is well worth the effort. Consider the following:
1. Own your videos. You should have the flexibility to be able to move your videos from one online location to another if you

need to. To maintain this control, be cautious about selecting video creation tools. Some applications will seem simple to use but the only way to view the videos created with their application is through their website; usually there is no way for you to download the videos that you created. Own your videos! It is also a good idea to create a backup copy of video files.

2. Invest in software that has the ability and flexibility to grow and adapt to changing needs. Think about the potential to collaborate with others on your videos and choose tools that would allow this to happen. There are a number of screen-recording applications available at a low or no cost, but as your video creation techniques grow you will want to consider tools that will allow you to do more with your videos.

3. Purchase hardware to create quality videos. This includes input tablet devices for annotating your videos and microphones to record clear audio. Audio is one of the most important factors in determining the quality of the video. Investing in dependable recording headsets is important.

4. Decide on a location to host and serve your videos. The main goal is to minimize, if not eliminate altogether, barriers to access. Remember your target audience. There is a good chance that they will be accessing these videos from a variety of locations and devices. Ensure that your videos will be not only easy to find, but will consistently play at high quality on a player that has simple navigation controls.

Plan for Success with Adult Learners

Regardless of the model, whether you choose to implement flipped faculty meetings or personalized flipped professional coaching, flipped learning requires intentional content. Digital content is only useful when it is accessible, relevant, and timely. And as teachers are typically very traditional learners, it is vital that you are thoughtful in your plans for using digital content with adults.

Accessible

Establish one location for information and drive your staff there every time you interact with them. Digital content should be accessible through a web-based platform. Consider the computer hardware that teachers have available to them, as well as Internet access throughout their classrooms and schools. Many educators will access content outside of the school day. Therefore, digital content needs to be hosted on a server/platform that is accessible outside of school grounds.

Minimize barriers for teachers who try and access the content. Create easy to remember sub-pages or short links for the website addresses of major landing pages. These landing pages should be webpages where you want your teachers to begin to access content—perhaps a login page for a learning management system or a school portal. Once teachers are logged in, it should be very clear where they need to go to access content. Consider the pros and cons of making content public. On one hand, public content requires no password and would be easily accessible by all of your staff. On the other hand, public content limits what you might be able to share. Many schools and districts create content that is specific to district applications, hardware, and workflow. These are things you might not want to be made public.

Show your teachers how they can learn through video. Many teachers can benefit from technical tips on how to view a tutorial video, from using the spacebar to start and stop the video (on many video players) to using the full-screen option when viewing the video. Do not underestimate the value of simple instruction.

Relevant
The use of digital content in the learning cycle is one of the most unique aspects of Flipped Learning. Digital content can take many forms and will vary based on the professional development model you choose to implement in your school or district. Over time, your video creation techniques will expand to include different styles and formats. Each video should be created around a specific audience and purpose. Consider the following approach to video creation:

Anticipate a need. Create videos on topic areas that you know your teachers will need. Along with tutorials, showcase real classroom examples or implementations relating to the topic. Cover the "how-to" basics of a variety of topic areas, from curriculum and classroom management to technology tools available in the district. These videos will be the foundation of your video library, but you will continually add more videos as new strategies, tools, or processes are adopted.

React to a need. Create videos for a specific purpose or need that arises in your conversations with teachers. For example, a teacher needs help getting students the necessary information on technology tools or processes in order to ensure success for a specific project. Step up and make that video. These videos can ensure the success of a project. Perhaps another teacher is interested in a specific instructional strategy to implement in the classroom. By reacting to that teacher's immediate need, you are able to provide intentional content for the teacher. The timing of the instruction, as well as a follow-up visit with a coach or mentor, can increase the likelihood of successful transfer of the learned skill into the classroom.

Celebrate success. Do not be afraid to capture a moment that you think could impact others. You probably have between two to four cameras on you at any one time (phone, iPad, computer, etc). Document important information and classroom moments that are shared by your teachers. Turn these source files into inspirational videos for sharing best practices and for celebrating both teacher and student success. Celebration videos can include interviews, classroom projects, student work and teacher conversations.

Be specific. It doesn't cost anything to capture and view digital film, and images can easily be deleted. So expand your reasons for creating a video to include short and simple directions or guidance for an audience of *one*. That's right. In the past, the cost of capturing and editing video prohibited us from even considering a video for just one person. We would aim to create videos that could be seen by anyone. Individual videos are created for one person in order to share information. This is especially helpful for individual professional coaching. Use simple, non-editable screen capture tools for quick and easy video creation that you can upload to a server and share with a link.

Timely
Teachers are busy, busy, busy. Unless they intentionally set time aside for self-directed professional development, you have another challenge of providing them with digestible morsels of meaningful information at the right time. When implementing flipped

professional development, you are asking teachers to extend the traditional experience to include self-directed learning. This is an area where teachers will need to be encouraged.

No matter what variety of Flipped PD that you choose to implement, consistency is important when it comes to content delivery. Since your flipped materials are important to the success of your face-to-face time, you must establish a method that is effective. This means that your content will not get lost in an email shuffle and teachers know how to access your materials. Decide upon a reasonable timeline for viewing the flipped materials, whether you send an email with the link to digital content, establish a web location that is updated on a regular basis, or both!

The Importance of Trusting Relationships
The more you get to know your teachers, the more you will understand what they need.

Flipped Learning is about the relationships between the coaches and the staff. Flipped learning requires this because the relationship between teacher and student is so important to both roles. As a coach, it's my obligation to listen to the teacher. Not only to gather clues for skill level, but also interests which lead to opportunity. In workshop settings in the flipped professional coaching model, much time is spent in conversation—negotiating plans and planning for timely delivery of resources—whether the resources are for inspiration, learning, sharing, or brainstorming. This is valuable time. Sharing stories of both success and failure will help teachers embrace a culture of learning, leading them to take risks and push towards innovation.

Teachers Are Courageous.
Model courageousness for students and teachers.
- **Raise your expectations for the culture of learning that you deserve as a professional.** If you are traditional in your own learning, you will most likely create a classroom culture of traditional learning. Do not be afraid of a non-traditional approach to learning.
- **Create your own professional learning network.** Connect with others around the world, making sure to follow

individuals who have opinions different from yours. Engage in professional conversation. Expand your ideas.

- **Be courageous in improving your own professional practice.** Participate in innovative teaching and learning practices for your own learning. Seek out new ideas from colleagues in your personal learning network. Be open to constructive feedback.

One of the most important parts of learning is the relationships between students and teachers, or teachers and professional colleagues or coaches. When we are a part of trusting relationships, we become more invested, dedicate ourselves to our professional work, and commit to growing for the good of the organization. The relationships that are created in a Flipped Learning environment are one of the biggest benefits of Flipped Learning.

Kristin Daniels is a former classroom teacher (middle school science) who transitioned into a technology integration role in 2006. Her passions are collaboration and innovation in the hopes of helping teachers to shift their thinking towards creating more student-centered classrooms and schools. She has a B.A. in Psychology from Northwestern University and an M.Ed in Elementary Education from DePaul University. She has been flipping professional development for teachers since 2011 by providing them with personalized digital resources and working with schools to create job-embedded, coaching opportunities during the school day. She is currently a member of the Flipped Learning Network, a non-profit organization created to provide educators with the resources they need to implement a flipped learning environment in their classroom. Her work on the board has provided her with many opportunities to engage in work with a variety of educators and organizations around the country. She believes that teachers are lifelong learners and should be given time and opportunity to connect with others. She believes that teachers have the desire to reflect on their patience and should be supported throughout the process. She believes that the greatest communities are created by individuals with a growth mindset and that this is something that can be nurtured.

Twitter: @kadaniels
Website: flippedpd.org

What is PLAYDATE?

Jennie Mageira Carolyn Skibba, Ben Kovacs,
Kristin Ziemke, Anita Huffman, Autumn Laidler
and Sue Gorman

PLAYDATE (People Learning and Asking "Y": Digital Age Teacher Exploration) is a new kind of conference. Think about the last time you attended a professional learning event. You probably left full of new knowledge and a list overflowing with new apps, programs, and skills to try out. Unfortunately, many of us lack the time and support to actually explore all of these new tools. Our lists grow longer and longer, yet tools that could transform our classrooms and empower our kids languish untested and unused.

PLAYDATE is a space for us to come together and collaboratively explore the tools we've always wanted to learn. The concept is to invite educators from around the area to join together on one day, sit in a room for a few hours, and just play. They collaborate to learn about EdTech apps, programs, and tools with one another. There are no presenters in the room, no experts, and no agenda; simply time to play, tinker, and explore.

This idea was hatched at 10,000 feet. In the fall of 2012, Anita Huffman, Autumn Laidler, Sue Gorman, and Jennie Magiera were flying home to Chicago from an EdTech conference. They left stimulated with new ideas and connections, their "to do" and "to try" lists brimming with new strategies, philosophies, and tools. As they floated on cloud nine onto the plane, they didn't let the end of the conference stop their collaboration and brainstorming. As the plane took off, so began two solid hours of edu-fun.

Soon they began to discuss the pros and cons of the past few conferences they had attended. They all agreed that they greatly valued meeting new educators and discussing the good gospel that is innovative technology use. And yet they also lamented that educators learn about a myriad of new tools, websites, tricks, and apps at these conferences only to go back to the "real world" and have little to no time (usually the latter) to ever master—or even simply explore—any of it.

Thus the idea of PLAYDATE was born. Jennie originally wanted to call it ExploriCON, but through iteration by Autumn and Sue, and the recurring idea of play, PLAYDATE came to be. After agreeing on a catchy moniker, together the group refined the idea to meet some unaddressed professional learning needs and leverage best practices seen at other conferences.

As soon as Anita, Autumn, Sue and Jennie returned home, they reached out their edu-thought partners: Ben Kovacs, Carolyn Skibba and Kristin Ziemke. Together, they worked to put on the first PLAYDATE in early 2013. By late 2014, the idea had spread to over three dozen events, five countries, and thousands of teachers. PLAYDATE continues to grow, allowing teachers around the globe to find the time to rediscover playtime and organically explore new ideas.

Check out the PLAYDATE website for more information. A PLAYDATE Do-It-Yourself form can be found at bit.ly/PLAYDATEDIY.

Please connect with and contact any of the PLAYDATE team using the Twitter handles below:

Jenny Mageira: @msmageira
Carolyn Skibba: @skibtech
Ben Kovacs: @kovacsteach
Kristin Ziemke: @kristinziemke
Anita Huffman: @msahuffman
Autumn Laidler: @mslaidler
Sue Gorman: @sjgorman

Facilitating Flipped PD For All Staff:
Bringing the Pieces Together
Laura Conley

Flipped PD is simply about being open to change. Giving teachers the opportunity and tools to engage allows teachers to seize the opportunity to be in control of their professional learning. My journey in developing flipped professional development began with an opportunity and the use of technology.

It began with a moment we have all been scared of: being called down to the principal's office. When I arrived at his office, he asked me to close the door for a chat. Little did I know at the time how my career was about to change. He needed someone to guide the staff in technology integration. He knew that technology integration was not his area of expertise, but he also knew how important it was to begin preparing teachers for the Common Core and the technology involved.

I'll admit, I was by far *no* expert, but when I was given the chance to do something I love—using technology in education—it was exhilarating and exciting. My principal knew that my passion and excitement could be contagious! By flipping professional development we are able to foster the same type of excitement for all teachers in the building. To do this, we must make them an integral part of the process and support them with the tools they individually need to be successful.

My goal in creating Flipped PD is to bring an engaging, teacher-centered, and technology-rich professional development to our staff. All technology is modeled beginning with an interactive agenda (an example at bit.ly/personalizedpd02). Teachers are asked a few weeks before the PD exactly what they need out of this session. Their agenda is centered on their needs as well as the principal's goals for each PD session. It is key to model all digital tools as a part of the daily learning environment and not as a separate tools. In doing so, this affords teachers an opportunity to see the possibility of how technology integration can engage students in the type of learning and technology use that is so much a part of their lives, both now and in the future.

To better understand how to flip professional development, you must begin with a better understanding of the role of the leaders of flipped professional development and how best to reach teachers and assist them in becoming even better professionals.

Five Keys to Successfully Flipped Professional Development
1. Have a Supportive Principal
2. Establish a Facilitator Mindset (Facilitating vs. Presenter)
3. Plan for Success
4. Implement Your Plan
5. Monitor, Adjust, and Follow-up

1. Have a Supportive Principal
The administrator is key in creating the interest, learning expectations, follow-up, and enthusiasm. I know that should go without saying, but this is incredibly important to the success of any professional development: to have the principal completely on board, seeing the value of creating engaging PD. With anything you are setting out to learn, there will always be room for improvement and a learning curve. Here are some key administrator components that I observed during the process of creating Flipped PD. This is by no means a complete list, but I think it will help you to begin thinking about what is required—whether you are the principal or facilitator.

11 Key Components for Administrators
1. It is important for the leader to model technology usage as much as possible. One step at a time is fine, but they must be an example of trying, failing, and trying again. This will go a long way with your teachers. Let them know it's okay to fail but to keep trying. Encourage facilitators to remember everyone has a beginning point. You will want a facilitator that is willing to openly share mistakes and the lessons

learned from those mistakes. It is also important for the facilitator to remember and give examples of what it was like when he/she started using technology. This will help others realize it's normal to learn by failure. After all, this is a team effort.

2. Be willing to pull others in to assist in areas that are not your strengths. It is typical to not know everything. If you are not an avid tech user, bring someone in or ask that techy person on your staff. There is almost always at least one person who would love taking the lead and sharing enthusiasm in technology integration.

3. Have a positive attitude about making changes. The let's-give-it-a-try attitude can be contagious!

4. Be attuned to the needs of the staff. If past professional development was not positive, or even dreaded, then be willing to listen to what the staff has to say about the success or failure of past PD. The staff will appreciate being asked for their input.

5. Collaboration must include all who are involved in facilitating the training. This allows everyone to be on the same page and keeps the expectations high.

6. Model the use of technology as the lead learner in the building. I know this can be very difficult. It takes a lot of time to learn the uses of technology. Start small. You may want to create a Twitter account and encourage teachers to do the same. Twitter is a great place for educational collaboration. There's so much available in the field of educational technology that no one can or ever will know it all.

7. Encourage all staff to begin using technology that best suits their lesson. If it doesn't enhance their lesson, it shouldn't be used. You might suggest using a tool for technology integration. A search will give you a selection of different models that will help your staff have a starting point.

8. Continue goal setting with all staff by encouraging specific growth. It's okay to be a beginner, but you don't want to *stay* a beginner.

9. Find more specific ways to encourage your staff, and make sure the more reluctant teachers are putting forth the effort to try new technology methods with their students. One suggestion would be to specify, "In the next nine weeks, if it makes sense within the context of enhancing your lesson, try to use technology such as engaging your students with an online response system." You may want to encourage teachers to try it several times, and analyze what worked, and what didn't work with their students during the nine weeks period. (I've included an example of an excellent free online response system later in the Implementing section.)

10. Having a plan in place for teachers to utilize the technology capabilities the school has to offer will make everyone more productive. While some teachers will encourage students to use technology in class, others may not allow devices to be turned on at all. By providing a concise plan of your expectations, teachers will be able to implement technology in their classroom on a more regular basis. We are in a digital age. This may be new to some of us, but it is everyday life to students.

11. Invest in a technology integration coach to be a daily guide for teachers and staff. The principal can not be everywhere. If funding is available, a technology coach can be the added support that your teachers need to get them started and keep them moving forward. To be clear, the technology coach will not have the same responsibilities as your IT department. To be the lead learner, a coach would need to demonstrate very strong people skills, understand everyone has a different starting point, and encourage teachers in their learning.

2. Establishing a Facilitator Mindset (Facilitator vs. Presenter)
Tapping into my previous experiences of attending traditional professional development helped me realize that this model could be improved upon greatly. I started questioning everything about the traditional model.

Did we want to be presenters or facilitators of learning? *Presenters* (in traditional professional development format) give their information to participants neatly packaged in their own style and view. The presenter is doing the work for you. *Facilitators* (in a flipped professional development format) design learning activities so that participants acquire knowledge and skill instead of just receiving it. I always prefer doing instead of sitting and listening, so I definitely wanted the PD to be engaging.

So how did our team (the curriculum coordinator, reading specialist, principal, and I) bring the professional development model together? We drew on our experiences as adult learners. From observing and being adult learners, we were aware of adult learning characteristics (*see below*). These characteristics will be found in most adult learners, so you will want to take these into consideration when working with your staff. We needed to also take into consideration the fact that everyone was at a different starting point or level of tech usage. From our collaboration concerning these traits and technology integration experience of the staff, we felt a facilitated professional development would be the best place to start. My principal's let's-give-it-a-try attitude was very helpful to fuel the energy for change.

Adult Learning Characteristics

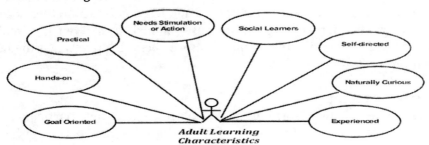

3. Planning for Success–Begin With the End In Mind

While thinking about the end result of creating an engaging professional development, there are numerous outcomes to be aware of. For instance, how many content areas could we address in this two-hour period and still allow time for teachers to practice, explore, and actively learn? How will we achieve learning?

Addressing the content areas, how many were too many? We started out with three. We quickly realized this was too many for the two-hour time period. Three different areas did not seem like much when we were planning, so I was a bit surprised when we couldn't fit everything in. It's hard to gauge how much time should be allowed, but when you have teachers engaged in fun learning, two hours goes by very quickly!

Prepare to Make Real-Time Adjustments
We had to make some adjustments during the session. It was starting to become evident that we would not have enough time to address everything we had planned. A couple of things were taking place, and as a facilitator, I could see a shift of topics happening during discussions. Since we were there to give the teachers what they needed we adjusted our agenda as the needs changed for more information about a particular subject area. For example, when a teacher asked about a tool to help with organizing information digitally, I suggested Evernote.com. Immediately, the group wanted more information. So we made a switch and provided more information about Evernote. After all, we had included links to all of the information so teachers could check out other tools that piqued their interests, but we wouldn't take time to discover these in the group session. These takeaways were intended for personal learning on their own. Teachers could explore the information or links to glean what best suited their students and lessons. We didn't want to give up the hands-on time because almost every teacher had expressed to me how important it was for them to have some time to explore.

Active Learning
We know active learning takes place when the participants (teachers) do most of the work. If I package the information, either on paper or on a virtual wall, and give it to the participants, even if I demonstrate everything, I am doing the work and not the participants. I would not be allowing the participants to be active learners. The instruction is important, but it should be designed so that the participants acquire the knowledge and skill rather than just receiving it from me.

We know in order for someone to learn something well, they must hear it, see it, question it, discuss it with their peers, and do it. It's also a good idea to teach it to someone else in order to better understand the information or skill. A good friend of mine once told me, "If I really wanted to be good at drawing, I should teach others to draw." She was absolutely right. After teaching drawing classes for several years to all ages, I could now completely understand an in-depth explanation of the process. When others came to me to learn to draw, I would never take the pencil from them to show them how to draw a certain component. I would instruct them, but they would be the active learner and doer.

Our Hurdles and How We Handled Them
Continuing to plan with the end in mind, there are a few hurdles to be cognizant of and be prepared for:

Does your school have enough bandwidth to support your flipped PD?
Our school was in the process of upgrading our technology infrastructure, so Wi-Fi was improving. This is essential, as the school will need substantial bandwidth and Wi-Fi support to properly function. It will be a process of seeing how much bandwidth is enough for different areas of the school. It could take some time for the IT staff to work this out, so be patient. The IT staff will be a valuable partner in technology integration in your school, so you will definitely want to cultivate your relationship with them.

Have you considered the advantages of working in a small-group setting for a more focused PD?
PD that is scheduled for all day with the entire staff, beginning with the first inservice when you return in the fall, is probably not the way anyone wants to spend a day. This whole-day PD can become very tiring and stressful, with a lot of time wasted waiting on others to create accounts, losing focus, and breaking off into off-topic conversations. A one-size-fits-all simply does not work. Knowing the results of these large-group PD sessions, we looked toward smaller, focused, departmental groups to alleviate some of the aforementioned results.

How will we develop positive relationships between the facilitators and the staff during PD?
Our traditional PD was given by a consulting company who often sent different presenters. As a result, no connection or relationship with the school staff was being created. With Flipped PD, the

facilitator will have had contact (via email or Google Docs, for example) with teachers before the session begins, so an opportunity for creating a relationship with the staff is available early on. Of course, if your facilitator is also a part of your staff, like I was, you will have the advantage of many strong relationships already established with colleagues.

If teachers are at varying levels of comfort with technology, how do we encourage growth in this area?
Be patient and supportive without allowing teachers to stay at the same level of integrating technology. Setting specific goals can help. Goals on usage—without setting limits on *which* tools teachers implement—is important to professionals. By allowing teachers the freedom to choose what is best for their needs, you validate their professional decision-making and empower the learning. For teachers with no experience in technology, another teacher could offer some suggestions on where to begin. If you have a technology integration coach, they will be able to give many suggestions, ideas, and tips for your teachers.

What digital tools will be of value to each classroom teacher?
We know this can be different with each teacher. We addressed the tools question by simply asking, *"What do you need?"* We found that most of the time, teachers didn't really know where to start or exactly what was available. We asked each teacher or group various questions about what they wanted or needed, but were also prepared to give suggestions to each group when they were unsure as to where to begin.

How much information can be shared in one PD session?
This is something that is very tough to do sometimes. I struggle with this question often. I want to share as much information as possible and get very excited about sharing technology integration tools with others, but I have to be careful not to overload the staff. Time has to be allowed for active learning! It can be very overwhelming, in particular, to the teachers new to using technology in their classrooms if you are sharing ten different resources in a short two-hour period. It's important to keep in mind that some have never integrated technology in their lessons, while others may use it frequently. It's very much like in your classroom. You have a diverse

group of students, and everyone is at a different level of understanding or usage of the knowledge they have acquired.

Respecting Teachers As Professionals–Asking for Teacher Input

When implementing your plan, receiving teacher input is essential. The method you use is not as important as getting the feedback from your staff. We chose to use email because all of our teachers were familiar with using it. When we emailed teachers, we did so in the groups they would be working in (see *below*). We grouped teachers by department to create as much common ground as possible so we could focus on each group's individual needs.

Good Morning,

We are preparing for your professional development scheduled for October 25. We want it to be all about your needs so we need and want your input!

If you have some specific areas you would like us to cover using iPads to enhance teaching and/or implementing Common Core we would like to here from you! Please reply sometime this week. *Each groups agenda can be different. Your group may want to focus on one of the suggestions below or something else entirely. We truly want this PD to be the best it can be for each group. So let us know as soon as you get a chance so we can be prepared to help you!*

A few of the areas we are considering:

- Socrative.com –An engaging student response system
- Using Splash Top apps to control your computer from your iPad
- Using infographics as a visual presentation tool
- Other apps for your subject area

Thanks so much,
Laura

A few things that proved helpful to us:
1. Grouping teachers with common needs (Departments).
2. Consider how long each PD session will be? We used chunks of time, usually about two hours per department, with rotating substitute teachers.
3. Meetings in the morning. Everyone was still fresh, more positive, and open to collaboration. We ruled out afternoons for all of the opposite reasons!
4. Each group had its own agenda, or plan of action, with specific needs.
5. Meeting in a conference room allowed more collaboration and working together was easier. In previous meetings we met in the library, but since we were meeting in small groups, we met in a conference room. With this shift, teachers were more focused, worked together more quickly, and were on task more often than when we met as a large group in the library. They didn't have the space to have side-bar conversations that didn't pertain to the session. This was a nice accident! Since it worked so well, we continued meeting in the conference room from that point onward.

All of these thoughts, ideas, and changes were important in establishing a professional learning team with our teachers. It is important for our teachers to know what the day will bring. They will come to PD better prepared and possibly with a more positive attitude. I wanted to set the tone as a team. If you were coaching or leading a football team, you wouldn't wait until the game started to let everyone know what your plans are for the day, so why wait to share the game plan for your PD session? After a few flipped PD sessions, teachers took ownership of their development and would contact me if they hadn't received their agenda within a few days of the upcoming PD session. I was glad that they had come to expect the information beforehand and that we were establishing a new tradition with our staff. Leading by our actions proved to our staff we valued everyone's time, which in turn expressed to teachers that we respected them as professionals.

4. Implementing Your Plan–Using Interactive Visual Agendas

Each group had its own agenda that was centered around their needs. Each group agenda was sent a few days *before* we meet and includes instructions on which tools we will be using, the content we will discuss, and anything else pertinent to their group. This advanced notice allowed everyone to be prepared and on the same playing field.

Teachers were asked to create accounts ahead of time for the web-based tools we would be using. This saves an enormous amount of time and frustrations. Teachers that are new to technology have the time to create accounts, think of login names, and passwords in their own space and time, without feeling pressured to hurry during the PD session. The ones who are more tech savvy appreciate not having to wait for everyone else to catch up. It is also meant to create an interest before the group meets. I wanted teachers to know what the day would bring, and I wanted them to be a part of it from the beginning.

Value Time
Time is the most precious commodity in the world. Using time wisely is important to all of us, as no one wants you to waste their time. Modeling all activities and instruction will show value in others' time.

One of the first ways we valued our staff's time was by creating interactive visual agendas. I decided that virtual agendas were the best option because paper agendas usually ended up in another stack of papers. They were simply pieces of paper with words and possibly instructions. They weren't visual or interactive in any way like the beautiful agendas we were using!

Everything on the agenda we were using was live-linked and just a click away. I hoped to eliminate the frustration teachers experienced in PD of figuring out what link we were using and then typing it in correctly. By embedding the links directly into our interactive agendas, this issue was completely avoided. Converting all teachers to these new, interactive agendas was not easy. We had one teacher in particular that was proud to be the only non-tech using teacher. Honestly, I don't know why he was proud of this, but he was. However, with every website and tool being linked and just a click away, he found success along with others without really trying. It was still obvious he clearly had little interest, but the interactive agenda gave him an easier, less confusing entry point.

By modeling the agenda to our staff, I was showing the usefulness of infographics in the classroom and appealing to the visual learner in the process. I used Piktochart.com, but there are many other tools to create infographics. Piktochart is a free, web-based tool that allows you access to it on any web-enabled device. It works best when used with Chrome or Firefox browsers. I found it easy to use even though there is some time involved while learning to use it to its fullest capacity. There are many other infographic creators available so you will want to choose the one that best suits your needs.

Piktochart agenda made interactive with Thinglink

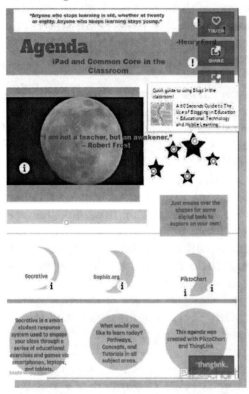

Modeling Technology for Teachers–Great Tools for Flipped PD

I began modeling by taking teachers through a short tutorial on infographics, then it was their turn to have the hands-on time. Time had been allotted for teachers to investigate making infographics while I was there to guide. One key concept to note here is to let the teachers be active learners and make mistakes. It's one of the best ways to really learn. Resist the urge to take the mouse and click for them. If they are struggling, they are learning. (I do, of course, encourage along the way!)

Thinglink

After teachers created their infographic they wanted to make it interactive with live links like the agenda sample. We used Thinglink.com to make this visual come to life with video or web links that appear when you mouse over that part of the image.

Thinglink is one of those fantastic tools that you are excited to use from the start. It's very quick to learn so it's perfect for beginners and experienced tech users alike. Once you upload the picture—or the infographic that you've created—you are just a few clicks away from adding the links.

Padlet

As we continued throughout the school year with Flipped PD, we modeled other digital tools. After creating visual agendas and modeling infographics, I began to find other digital resources that I would use for agendas and to demonstrate their usefulness in the classroom. Another great visual agenda tool I discovered was Padlet.com. Using Padlet as a virtual wall was a great, new option, as I was able to include all of our PD resources in one place. Padlet quickly became a favorite among teachers for several reasons: It is user-friendly, intuitive, versatile enough for both students and teachers, and if you are only posting comments, you do not have to create an account.

Virtual walls are simply a spot to park all of the session information so that it is easily accessible to everyone. Users are able to collaborate in real-time with Padlet. For instance, teachers could use it to create a group wall for their department. If you work in the math department, one person could create a wall and set the privacy so that only the teachers in the math department are the only ones who can access this wall and information. They could add resources, ideas, and tips to share with colleagues. If you want to share something that works well in your class, it just takes a couple of minutes to post it on the wall. With this type of collaboration teachers can work together without being in the same room and can choose the time that is right for them. If you are working at home, the wall can be accessed for your convenience anytime day or night.

This flipped-style of professional development can become a very time-saving method of collaboration and sharing of great lessons and ideas. One of the teachers I work with told me how after our flipped PD session, she decided to create links to all of the websites she uses on a regular bases in her class using Padlet. She decided it would be a quick visual and easy to edit with just a couple of clicks on her wall. She left this wall private for her own personal use, but can open it to others if she chooses at any time. Other teachers shared ideas about students using Padlet for projects. A history teacher used it with his high school students to replace the ever-famous poster board projects. His students could change the background of the wall to act as a backdrop for their project. They could work together, without being together physically, freeing them to work at any time but still as a team. The greatness of flipped PD lies in the resources being introduced and modeled, and then teachers using these resources in their classrooms.

Pyron Elementary virtual wall of PD resources using Padlet.

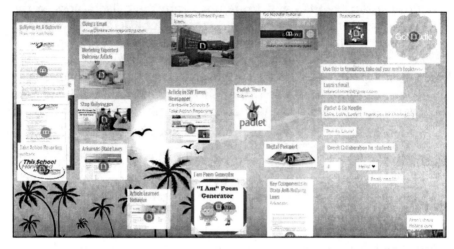

5. Monitor, Adjust, and Follow up
Monitor

Actively being aware of what's going on in the room as you facilitate a session is advantageous in using time efficiently and keeping participants on task. This can be accomplished by remembering adult learning characteristics, using classroom management skills, being knowledgeable about the content areas you are facilitating, and having a presence where needed to encourage teamwork. Monitoring and being ready to quickly and seamlessly make adjustments, without teachers being aware you are doing so, will ensure a productive PD time.

Be Prepared to Adjust

The first time we tried flipping our PD, I was very nervous. I wanted everything to go perfectly like I had it visualized in my head, and that was my first mistake. The facilitation went very well, but not exactly like I had it planned. During my first session of PD, I needed to be responsive to groups 1, 2, and 3 and had to make an adjustment.

Teachers arrived with the accounts created for the session, their laptops or iPads, and were ready to start. We were off to a good start, and I could sense all of the positive attitudes in the room. Being in the conference room provided a more intimate setting, and everyone was comfortable with snacks and drinks. (Food is always a plus!) The smaller work area was perfect for conversations across the table and seem to be contributing to keeping these conversations on topic.

My computer was connected to the smart board when, thirty minutes into the session, the Wi-Fi went down. This could happen anywhere and anytime, so we should have been prepared with a back-up plan. Our district had just completed a major project of updating the Wi-Fi throughout our schools, so I assumed we wouldn't have any issues. It was not a wise assumption, but we were meeting in the superintendent's conference room, so I was sure everything would work in there. As facilitators we had to adjust our plan and use this teachable moment. While trying not to panic, we talked briefly about this happening in class. How would you deal with this issue? What is your backup plan or is winging it a plan? Could your students be a part of this teachable moment if this or other tech issues happened while teaching with technology? We were working with teachers at the high school level who have more opportunities to engage the students as part of the solution. Your students could be your greatest resources, as your technology concern could be something they have worked with or fixed on their own. This could be an opportunity for a student to share his/her computer skills. This simple adjustment finds a new way for engagement to take place and also turns the tables and allows students to take charge of learning to some degree. Personally, I love learning from our students and watching the confidence that builds from these experiences.

All groups were very similar. Only one teacher admitted he didn't have his accounts created ahead of time and he quickly took care of that before everyone else arrived. Being able to adjust to teachers' needs will save time and frustrations for everyone involved.

Feedback–The Value of Following Up

To me, follow-up is as important as the planning ahead process. Using timely feedback, we know some of their thoughts from before, during, and after the session. It brings the group and the facilitation full circle. As facilitators, we used the post-meeting surveys to determine areas we could improve upon and more specific subjects our teachers needed assistance with, and as a guide for choosing the digital tools for upcoming professional development sessions.

Socrative

In preparation for our PD meeting, we created a brief survey using Socrative.com. Socrative is a free, engaging, web-based, student response system. We used Socrative to not only gather the information we wanted, but also to continue modeling and connecting tools to applicable uses in the classroom. From our modeling and use of Socrative, teachers found it to be a tool they could use right away in their classroom. We asked our teachers the following questions:

1. Was the pre-workshop communication valuable to the outcome of today's PD?
2. Thinking of the information presented, did you feel it was relevant to your needs?
3. Did the facilitators explain and then allow time for you to practice or have hands-on time?
4. Overall, how satisfied were you with this model of professional development?

Socrative questions and results from the first groups.

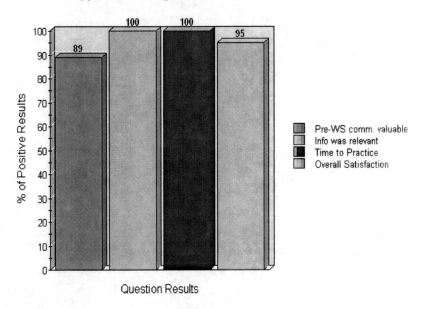

Flipped PD Survey Results

SurveyMonkey

We continued to follow up throughout the school year with quick four-question surveys via SurveyMonkey. SurveyMonkey.com is another free, web-based tool that allows users to engage their participants via a survey shared through a link. This link can be emailed, embedded, or distributed through social media.

Our survey was emailed to staff approximately two months after the first flipped PD session. Question 2 asked, "How often do students use the netbooks in your class?" This survey was anonymous to allow the staff the ability to provide candid answers to each question. The answers provided us with a quick assessment of regular usage of netbooks in class. The results are shown below.

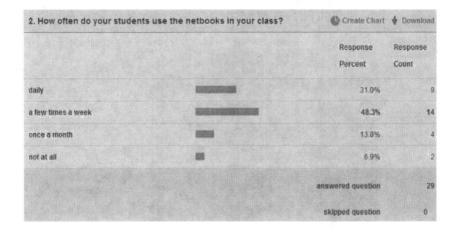

Question 4 asked, "Is there a specific 'digital tool' that you've seen or heard about and would like to learn more about its uses for your classes?" The answers seem to indicate that teachers are unsure of what they need or possibly what is available. From the answers on this question, we knew to continue with suggesting technology integration tools to the staff.

All surveys are used to follow-up on a more individual basis. From the first anonymous survey results, I realized that some questions, like Question 4, needed to be asked without anonymity. I continued alternating between these two types of surveys. I continually learn and adjust the questions and types of surveys in order to be the best facilitator possible.

I would use the survey information to directly contact teachers to setup a time to work one-to-one with them. From the surveys and these conversations, I would guide teachers in integrating new technology with their students during class. The teachers gained new skills with less stress than going at it alone, and it is always a joy to work directly with students and technology. It's great to see students excited and engaged during a lesson. At our high school, students are always glad to jump in and help if you are having tech issues as well. It's fun to learn from the students, too!

We use each survey's results to prepare for the next professional development session. This process of continually asking for feedback is what ensures our professional development is addressing the needs of our staff.

Bringing it all together
With the information from our experiences and your knowledge of the needs of your staff or colleagues, it's time for you to begin thinking about the changes you would want to see in professional development. Your school may have completely different needs or some very similar, but hopefully I've given you the advantage of a starting point.

I look forward to hearing about your Flipped PD experiences. You may email me, and I will always respond! I can also be found on Twitter and my website.

Personalized PD

Laura Conley spent the past three years creating and sharing her ever- changing model of professional development. Like many things in life, it was created out of necessity! She was given an opportunity to work closely with principals, teachers, and the district staff, while sharing technology integration tools with teachers. It was through this seized opportunity that her version of Flipped PD began!

She has written articles about flipping professional development for magazines, blog posts, and shares information through various podcasts. She is an active presenter at national conferences for technology integration in education.

Her passion for technology, combined with her skills working with adults and students has energized school staff and students to engage and navigate the latest technologies in schools today. She is a technology integration facilitator with her company Flipped-PD, LLC working with schools across the US.

Twitter: @lconley86
Website: flipped-pd.com
Email: takeactiontech@gmail.com

What are #SummerLS & #EduLS?
Todd Nesloney

In March of 2014, I was hired as the Principal/Lead Learner of Navasota Intermediate in Navasota, Texas. As part of my becoming the new leader, I had to hire an entirely new staff. I spent the next two months doing just that. As summer approached, I began to think about ways that I could encourage my brand new team to learn even before we all came together. Ever since I began networking on Twitter in 2012, I knew the value of connecting with and learning from others. So I cooked up the idea of a "Summer Learning Series" (or the #SummerLS on Twitter).

My very first challenge for my new staff was creation of their own twitter accounts. We were going to be a school that would learn from others around the world, as well as share our own stories. After sending out this challenge to my staff, a twitter friend saw the YouTube video I had made showing how to set up a Twitter account. They loved it and wanted to share. Then they wanted to know if they could follow along and learn with us! Several other twitter friends saw that conversation and asked to join in, too. So I figured, *Why not open the Summer Learning Series up to everyone?*. And I did just that.

As I was creating challenges, I realized that the biggest thing I was trying to show my staff was the power of connection. And what better way to teach that then to actually use some of my many friends from around the world to help design challenges? So I reached out to tons of my friends (including Dave Burgess, Angela Maiers, Eric Sheninger, Jennifer LaGarde, Ben Gilpin, Brad Gustafson, Amber Teamann, and so many more), and they all designed challenges. As the learning series grew, I was blown away. What started as a learning series for my 16 teachers, turned into a learning series for almost 3,000 in 7 different countries! It was mind-blowing to say the least.

I ended the #SummerLS right before school started as I began to focus more heavily on the day-to-day concerns of my new job. Then in late November, I was notified that #SummerLS had been nominated for an EduBlog Award for Best Open PD. What? I couldn't believe people were still talking about my little ol' Summer Learning Series. As the votes began to pour in (and as we ended up *winning* the category), I was inspired to bring the #SummerLS back as a year-long learning series!

And from that experience the "Educator Learning Series" (#EduLS) was born...or *reborn*. I can't wait to see where this is going to take us on our learning journeys, but I am so thrilled to be able to help even more teachers realize their potential and see all the great ways that people are teaching and working with kids from all around the world. Because in the end, we are only as good as the people with whom we surround ourselves, so why not surround yourself with the best?

What I love most about doing something like this is that anyone can do this! Never would I have thought of myself as someone who could lead an entire summer of professional development. But I stepped out on a limb, asked a few friends to help, and watched awesomeness happen. Educators are so busy and money is so tight in many districts that, as instructional leaders, we have to continue thinking of new and innovative ways to make sure that our team is consistently learning and growing. So what are you waiting for? Start the journey today!

Check us out on educatorlearningseries.blogspot.com

Todd Nesloney is the Principal/Lead Learner of Webb Elementary in Navasota, TX. He formerly taught 4th and 5th grade for 7 years at Fields Store Elementary in Waller, Texas. He is the 2014 Bammy Award Recipient for Elementary Classroom Teacher of the Year, the TCEA Teacher of the Year for 2014, a White House Champion of Change, a National School Board Association "20 to Watch", Center for Digital Education "Top 40 Innovators in Education", Classroom Champions Teacher, and part of the Remind Teacher Advisory Board. Todd also is the co-founder of The 3 Tech Ninjas education technology training company, the author of children's book "Spruce & Lucy" and the co-author of the Award Winning Book, "Flipping 2.0: Practical Strategies for Flipping Your Class". He is also the co-host of the popular, top iTunes rated, education podcast series "EduAllStars".

Twitter: @TechNinjaTodd
Website: toddnesloney.com

Empowered Learning
Dr. Brad Gustafson

I'm sure we've all experienced a traditional staff meeting or professional development workshop that left us feeling diminished. If you're anything like me, you have probably even planned a meeting that missed the mark. Unproductive meetings are disappointing to everyone involved. Participants feel captive because the structure of traditional meetings can be unresponsive to our natural inclination to learn and be social.

Teachers are professional learners. When teachers are placed in supportive environments that are responsive to their natural inclination to learn and grow, their capacity to effectively meet the needs of students also increases. Conversely, when teachers are subjected to environments that restrict their professional needs, a negative impact to teachers and subsequently student learning could result. A similar scenario can be observed in nature.

Orca whales are social animals that can grow dorsal fins reaching six feet in height. However, their fins collapse in captivity because the fibrous tissue that makes up an orca's dorsal fin is not reinforced. When teachers experience a PD meeting that doesn't reinforce their needs, they too can feel deflated. Principals serving as "lead learners" must nurture a reverence for learning in their staff. Flipping PD is an empowering approach that fosters learning in a manner that represents current best practice.

The approach has allowed our school to supplant a regular staff meeting each month with powerful PD options that are responsive to our teachers' needs. Truth be told, the monthly PD breakout session choices feel more like a choose-your-own-PD-adventure than a typical meeting or workshop. Our teacher-leaders and breakout session facilitators have repurposed our time together as a staff.

F.L.I.P.: The Acronym that Embodies Empowered Learning

In most dictionaries the term "flip" is described as turning something over swiftly, or a sudden movement. I would describe the transformation of our staff meetings the past few years as a subtle shift, not a sudden flip. PD does not exist in a vacuum. That is to say, we cannot reinvent PD without considering its context. For us, it made the most sense to start flipping staff meetings slowly in order to eventually move faster. For us, it's become all about the Focus, Learning, Inclusion, and Purpose.

An overview of the F.L.I.P. acronym and several guiding questions are provided below. This is just enough information to get you started, while later in the chapter you'll be provided in-depth information to support your efforts to more fully empower staff learning. By addressing each of the preliminary guiding questions below in your PD planning, you can empower staff learning and break free from traditional, unidimensional, or restrictive PD approaches.

F: Focus

Professional development should be focused on school goals. Limit the number of goals your school has to three or fewer. Avoid the temptation to focus on too many things.

Ask yourself the following guiding questions to achieve greater focus in flipping PD:

- What is the focus for our time?
- How does this focus connect to specific school goals?
- Am I sending mixed-messages to staff by focusing on too many things?

L: Learning

Empower staff by asking them what professional development they need. Ask for feedback and hold yourself to the highest standard when planning professional development.

Ask yourself the following guiding questions to prioritize staff learning when planning PD:

- What are the learning targets?
- How will student learning be improved as a result of this PD?
- What have my past failures in this area taught me about moving forward?
- What do I need to learn to do a better job meeting staff needs or flipping PD?
- If this meeting was optional would our staff show up? Why or why not?

I: Inclusive

Give staff choice and voice in their learning to ensure everyone is valued. Include different employee groups in every stage of the PD planning process. Honor the varying background experiences and readiness levels of staff when planning flipped PD.

Ask yourself the following guiding questions to include all staff in professional development:

- Who might need something more, or different?
- How can I be more inclusive?
- How might I empower staff to take ownership of their learning through this experience?
- Am I giving every staff member a voice?
- How will I collect and use staff feedback about our PD?
- Is this content and format serving all staff?

P: Purpose

Purpose is distinctly different from focus. Your purpose for meeting will drive the approach you take. This approach will facilitate staff interaction with a meeting's focus. For example, your purpose for a PD experience could be to model an innovative instructional strategy to staff or to maximize face-to-face time at a meeting. With the purpose identified, you will then plan an approach that supports staff learning around a specific goal or focus. Always start by identifying the purpose for PD meetings and plan the format accordingly.

Ask yourself the following guiding questions to ensure you're being purposeful in your PD planning:

- What is the core purpose for this PD experience?
- How might this purpose be achieved?
- Are there other innovative approaches I haven't considered to realize this same purpose?
- How is the purpose of this meeting or PD experience distinctly different from its focus?

Screenshot from a flipped PD video used at the district level. The video was created using the TouchCast app.

3 Steps to Flipping PD

Flipping PD is as easy as 1, 2, 3. After reading this entire chapter, be sure to revisit the following three steps:

1. *Share a video or article with your staff before a meeting.*

Create or curate the information you want to provide to staff. If you choose to create a video, I suggest using the TouchCast App. At this time, TouchCast is still a free app, and it features a user-friendly interface. It is easy to upload links and photos to TouchCasts, and best of all the app limits videos to five minutes. However, flipping PD with videos is not the only way to enhance staff learning; sharing resources like articles, blog posts, graphics, and research can be an effective form of flipped PD, too.

- To learn more about TouchCast, go to touchcast.com
- See a sample TouchCast video here bit.ly/personalizedpd04

2. *Get together to discuss the video or article.*
The best reason to flip PD is to maximize your face-time together. Let staff work in small groups together after watching a flipped PD video or reading some research you've provided ahead of time. Be sure to plan some form of face-to-face follow-up that promotes sharing and reflection.

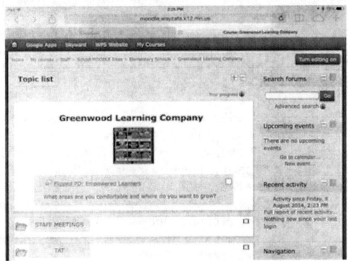

Screenshot from our school Moodle page. The benefit of collecting feedback in a shared online forum is that staff can see colleagues' needs and feedback can be referenced over time to ensure it is being used to guide PD planning.

3. *Collect feedback that will guide your next PD iteration.*
Use the feedback to improve the process for staff. Persevere! Feedback can be collected in multiple ways including 1:1 conversation, a traditional form like the one we've used for our breakout sessions, or an interactive online forum like our school's

Moodle site. Regardless of how you collect feedback, our students and staff are relying on us to model grit and a growth mindset.

A Catalyst for Change
When I first heard about flipped instruction, I knew I wanted to learn more. I also wanted to understand how it helped students learn. I recognized that I had a responsibility to support our school in exploring the innovative approach through effective modeling. I approached this topic as a learner and began exploring how flipped instruction might enhance our PD experiences.

We started flipping portions of our staff meetings a couple years ago, and the ethos in our school has changed noticeably over time. How we "do PD" and approach staff meetings has made a difference! It's not that I executed the approach to flipping or blended learning flawlessly; I assure you it was quite the contrary. I recall flipping meetings that had no business being flipped. I also did my share of supplanting face-to-face meetings with digital content without regard for the critical element of human interaction that meetings can fulfill. One such instance was an annual fall meeting in which teachers were to meet their new peer coaches.

Our peer coaches are tasked with partnering with teachers to foster reflection and professional growth. The entire process requires trust, and that trust is built over time. In my haste towards efficiency, I converted one of these introductory peer coaching meetings to a video-recorded format without building in a face-to-face experience. This left our peer coaches and teachers yearning for something that viewing a video can't provide. Our early learning with flipped meetings did produce some positive results, and we did do some foundational things really well.

We have exemplary teacher-leaders involved with PD planning. We focused on our school goals, protected our learning time together, included all staff, and were purposeful in the process. In a positive and dramatic paradigm shift, teachers are now our go-to PD facilitators. PD is viewed as something that's *for* us and not something that's done *to* us. We've found ways to maximize our time (a precious commodity these days) while honoring the busy schedules of our staff. The process of integrating the flipped approach into PD has been iterative with plenty of failures along the way; I've embraced these because with each misstep we reflected upon what we really wanted our learning to look like.

Through the meaningful integration of technology, it is possible to flip staff meetings and empower teachers in their professional learning. A twenty-first century paradigm for PD is emerging, and it's leading to newfound personalization, professional freedom, and inspiration. This innovative practice empowers teachers to own their learning and go deeper than the traditional PD experience allows.

School Culture

Many variables influence a school's culture. Since we started applying the tenets of the F.L.I.P. acronym, we've seen a dramatic increase in employee engagement. In three years of trend data collected from our school staff using the K-12 Insight's standardized survey instrument, we've realized a 12% increase in teachers who are highly engaged and a 21% increase in paras and clerical staff that are highly engaged. In a school with more than 100 staff members, these increases offer compelling data that translate into real people...real people that work directly with our students on a daily basis!

The increasing levels of employee engagement seem palpable at times, and one of the most rewarding byproducts of our flipped PD meetings is that I'm seeing the approach carried over into flipped classroom instruction. A change in practice is emerging as classroom teachers have also begun flipping instruction. I've observed a more constructivist student learning experience as a result. Fifth grade social studies lessons are coming alive because talented teachers are using flipped instruction to maximize student contact time. Students are assigned reading at home instead of going over new content together in class. Students arrive at school the following day and post a reflection to Moodle in an online forum. Next, they read and interact with their classmates in the forums. This flipped instruction frees up additional class time for theater, debates, and other collaborative projects related to the content. The bulk of class time is now spent on engaging activities to extend students' learning.

The interest in flipping is spreading as students are experiencing success in our school. This was one of my original goals when introducing the flipped approach at some of our initial staff meetings. I modeled the approach hoping that staff would see value and apply it in a way that made sense for their students. Since that time, the district has also provided some training, and teachers have been involved in classes taught by colleagues. Now, I find myself learning alongside teachers that are flipping instruction and applying successful strategies they're using to flipped PD. I'm also able to better support their efforts because I've been immersed in the same work and learning around flipped instruction for a couple years. The support recently manifested in a teacher observation post-conference.

I was meeting with a staff member, and we were discussing many of the phenomenal things that occurred as a result of the flipped lesson format she used. We also discussed next steps including scaffolding students' online forum responses to foster critical thinking and more depth in their comments. During the observation, we had noticed that students loved interacting with one another and providing online feedback to peers. However, occasionally students responded, "That's awesome" without offering specific connections to the text or their partner's writing. The result of our post-conference conversation was a tool designed to power up digital learning. See it here: bit.ly/personalizedpd06

The tool is based on Bloom's Taxonomy and gets progressively more involved as a student works his way towards the bottom of the tool. Our shared experiences with utilizing the flipped approach contributed to my being able to offer more tangible support and responsive feedback.

A Deeper Look: How to Flip your Professional Development
Before you start recording videos and calling it "flipped PD," be sure to reflect upon the principles below. When you and your staff are ready to flip your PD, apply the tenets of the powerful F.L.I.P. acronym to create conditions for teachers to thrive as professional learners.

F	**Focus**: Focus on what matters. Explicitly identify why it matters and make a clear connection to specific school goals. Then, fan the flames to reignite your faculty's love for professional development. Create staff meeting experiences that are so coherent and focused that staff can easily identify the value.
L	**Learning**: It's all about the learning. That's it! Learning should be revered, and teachers deserve championship-caliber learning experiences. If your staff meetings and site PD is only "good", it's time to make some mid-game adjustments. Let's make PD something that is *great*! Collaborate with your staff to plan a PD comeback.
I	**Inclusive**: Include all staff. If your school's PD doesn't include hooks for all staff...something is fishy! If your PD planning is too complex and there's more emphasis on the bells & whistles than the guiding questions, you need to scale it back. Keep it simple and you'll have everyone on board.
P	**Purpose**: Purpose drives PD. Identify the PD problems you want to address and go after them in an unswerving manner. As staff learning gains momentum, your purpose will likely change; watch for these changes, and be prepared to recalibrate how/what you're flipping to keep PD responsive to staff needs.

Focus Ignites Learning

How to focus when flipping:
1. Start by identifying a few school goals. (Do not exceed three goals.)
2. Be sure that each PD experience focuses on one of the three goals your school has identified.
3. At the beginning of a flipped PD video or face-to-face staff meeting, share a learning target or guiding question with staff. This will provide clarity and focus on essential learning.

In order to successfully flip staff meetings, principals must establish a focus and communicate meeting priorities and anticipated outcomes with staff. Flipping a staff meeting should not be seen as something "extra" that is being piled onto an already exhaustive initiative list. Instead, flipping a faculty meeting should enhance learning by making the link between PD and school goals crystal clear. Without a clear focus on essential learning even the most well-intentioned PD plans will fall to pieces.

Anyone that has ever assembled a Lego set from miscellaneous, scattered pieces understands the importance of focus. Hunting for a specific plastic piece becomes an even more daunting task once the plastic bricks have been combined with remnants from multiple toy sets. My son was recently constructing a toy Lego dragon and he needed my help searching for a translucent orange "fire" piece. (After all, what good is a Lego dragon without a flame?!) Being a self-proclaimed Lego maniac, I was happy to oblige. A lifetime of Lego building has taught me the critical skill of being able to focus on a particular color when searching for specific pieces. The moral of the story is simple yet profound; whether you are searching for a translucent orange Lego "fire" brick or meaningful PD, focus is critical. As a principal, we can serve our staff by maintaining focus on school-wide goals so that the myriad of extraneous "pieces" don't distract us from providing phenomenal professional development.

We have harnessed the power of focus as a school. Our staff approaches PD by focusing on *three goals each year*. Our PD experiences connect to these goals, and meetings that are flipped should also support school goals. Focus transcends format.

For example, in planning any type of PD (flipped or traditional sit-and-get), it's important to provide focus. We do this by establishing our school goals annually and in a collaborative manner. Our site data team is comprised of teacher-leaders representing every grade-level and department. We spend a portion of the summer reviewing assessment data and discussing our building's unique needs and context. From these conversations emerge three school focus areas; these foci inform our goals. All PD supports our school's goals. Here's how it works...

The goals our data team identified this past school year were:
1. High student achievement in literacy
2. Meaningful technology integration
3. Positive relationships

I will be unpacking the first goal to help principals better understand the process we used in planning PD and flipping some staff meetings. My intent is not to expound upon all three of our school goals, but to highlight the importance of focus when flipping. The important thing to remember is to focus PD on school goals and limit the number of goals you have to three or less.

In looking at our first goal, high student achievement in literacy, we developed a SMART goal as one metric:

The percentage of all students enrolled October 1 in grades 3-5 at Greenwood Elementary School who earn an achievement level of Meets the Standards or Exceeds the Standards in reading on all state accountability tests (MCA, MTAS, MOD) will increase from 80.6% in 2013 to 82.6% in 2014.

After our school SMART goal was established, grade-level teams took ownership by developing goals for their students. The process empowered staff to lend their voice and experience into how their PLC time would be spent. It also enabled each team to establish a laser-like focus on an element of student learning/achievement that they determined to be a difference-maker for kids.

One year we had a team achieve their grade-level goal on the very last day of school. The teachers had aspired to help 100% of students reach a particular benchmark with 80% accuracy or better, and— with targeted interventions, focus, and lots of heart—they made it. It felt as if the entire school celebrated along with the team when this goal was met; it was awesome!

In addition to the job-embedded PD our PLCs are involved with, we structured two consecutive months of flipped PD to support learning around literacy and the Common Core State Standards (CCSS). There was a direct link to our school goals, and the structure of the flipped PD supported deeper engagement within the CCSS. The research and resources that staff had online access to included six articles and one video. Staff members were asked to select from these resources and reflect on a guiding question that the flipped PD focused upon. Teachers were also asked to respond to 2-3 forum posts from colleagues. The guiding question we used is below, and it was focused on addressing our first school goal.

Q. Based on the Common Core State Standards (CCSS) what teaching and learning shifts are necessary to move students towards "College & Career" ready?

Each and every staff member's voice mattered, and by leveraging flipped PD in a focused manner we could more effectively collaborate together. Teachers' questions and comments were authentic and prompted me to reflect on how I can better support our staff in implementation of the CCSS. Forum responses from teachers exemplified scholarship and a commitment to learning. Some themes that emerged that I found especially helpful as a principal were:

- Teachers reflected on how our district curriculum addresses the CCSS shift towards a greater emphasis on process as opposed to content.
- Questions surfaced about how we might create student learning experiences for real audiences with real purposes.
- Staff inquired about support they will receive in implementing the adoption of CCSS.

Due to time constraints and other factors, there are times when conversations at staff meetings are dominated by a vocal minority. Flipped PD that is focused provides all staff members a voice in the learning process.

As next steps to our flipped PD sessions and online forum postings about CCSS, we circled back to the same topic the following month. This continuation builds cohesion between PD meetings and helps cement the focus for a school year. We held a face-to-face breakout session with two guiding questions about the CCSS for continuity. A similar cohesive approach was used for our school's other goals.

To address our focus on positive relationships we planned an all staff Honor Retreat at the beginning of the school year. This workshop celebrated the amazing work our teachers and paraprofessionals do on a daily basis. We followed up during subsequent months with breakout sessions on the Responsive Classroom approach led by staff and flipped PD on Cultural Proficiency. All of these experiences were focused on our priority of positive relationships.

As a principal, it is critical to support teachers by providing focus. When a staff understands the goal, they can more effectively take the next steps to deliver for kids. On the contrary, if clarity is lacking, PD will feel like a moving target or wandering magnifying glass. Make sure your flipped PD is focused.

We kept the focus on our school goals this past winter when we planned a flipped PD series. The flipped PD was our kick-off to some spring breakout PD sessions led by staff. (Go to bit.ly/personalizedpd08 to see a copy of our flipped PD and Breakout Session Options.)

In planning the flipped PD series, we intentionally scaled back staff meetings during those winter months to ensure that the flipped PD was not viewed as piling on additional work. Focus can be compromised if we allow our staff to be inundated with too many meetings or demands on their time. There are other factors that can potentially diminish flipped PD.

Do not flip staff meetings and PD without reflecting on the value of face-to-face conversation and follow-up. In planning the flipped PD session on culturally proficient teaching, we were reminded that flipped PD should maximize face-to-face time in meetings and not supplant it. We scheduled time for teachers to come together to discuss the material together. I was part of these conversations and was inspired by the commitment, care, and authenticity of staff.

Personally, reading the research and watching the videos in advance had a positive effect; it disarmed some of my own bias and initial knee-jerk responses by allowing me to personally reflect on my own journey with culturally-proficient teaching. This translated into being able to listen and ask better questions when we were together as a staff. The research and videos that staff interacted with in the flipped meeting format led to deeper conversations that we had not previously experienced in traditional staff meetings. The same can be said of some of the dialogue that was exchanged asynchronously on our school's staff Moodle site.

One teacher posted a response that included some connections she had made to her Master's program and a poem by Paul C. Gorski called, "Becoming Joey." I think it's important for principals to see

103

the *reward* that is possible when flipped PD is used in a manner that amplifies teacher voice:

"I am in my Master's program right now and just completed a class based on this very topic. One of the main points I took away from the class was the impact that a teacher's behavior has on students. We discussed 15 behaviors from TESA (Teacher Expectations and Student Achievement) training. I won't list them all, but the one that stood out the most was Personal Regard. Students who felt like their teacher cared for them and took an interest in them, regardless of academic ability, race, or socioeconomic status, achieved more. This regard can be done through simple chats, eye contact, smiling, and generally showing interest in students. As I watched the video, Culturally Responsive Teaching, I thought of a poem we also discussed in my program, called Becoming Joey, about a boy who suppresses his Mexican culture to fit in at his predominantly white school:

Becoming Joey
By Paul C. Gorski via EdChange.org
Jose's ten.
Looks six by size,
twenty in the eyes.

Down
the school-morning street
he ambles along
dotted lines of busses and cars
that spit exhaust like expletives,
disturbing his meditation
on a few final moments of peace.

He is frail but upright.
Hand-me-downs hang from his slenderness,
Patched and stained.
Soles flop beneath battered shoes,
Worn through but hanging on,
If only by one lace.

He pauses in the schoolyard
where white kids laugh and scurry
unaware of this, his battle;

of this, his burden; of this, his borderlands.
Behind him; cracked sidewalks
and frosty nights
sweetened by the warmth of belonging.
Before him; manicured playgrounds,
heated classrooms,
and enthusiastic lessons about a world
that doesn't see him.

Still he moves forward,
what feels in his stomach
a regressive sort of forward.
And he straightens his shirt,
tries dusting off the stains of ancestry.
And he clears his throat,
tries spitting out his Mexican voice.
And, becoming Joey, he crosses into school.

Other staff members responded to the poignant post and message within the poem with personal reflections. The interactions were incredibly impactful and represented one of nine discussion threads on the topic. I'll be the first to admit that the traditional, mundane meetings I facilitated prior to adhering to the F.L.I.P. acronym never elicited poetry submissions and focused dialogue like this. Principals are in a unique position to empower their staff, and in doing so we put teachers in a better position to make a difference for kids.

It's important to note how flipped PD does not drive school goals, but rather our focus drives all PD. The flipped staff meetings and PD were planned to *support* the important work we do! Notice how we did NOT start by saying we were going to flip every single staff meeting and set goals that aligned with a flipped staff meeting approach. We used flipped PD as one tool to enhance our focus on school priorities.

There was a sustained effort to engage staff in interacting with each priority over the course of the year. As part of this effort, we collaborated with staff and developed a series of personalized PD experiences that spanned several months. Each month staff would have multiple breakout sessions to choose from. Within these breakout session options, there was also some tiering and additional scaffolding depending on the technology involved.

> ****Flip-Tip for Admin:** *Model best practice whenever you are flipping a staff PD experience. Identify the learning target(s) and guiding questions so staff can identify the focus right away.*

By flipping instruction you can rekindle spirits and increase focus on school priorities.

I recommend that you approach PD as a sustained experience and not a single event or meeting. The integration of flipped PD within this context will supercharge and accelerate the learning, instead of being viewed as an interruption. These focused experiences should build upon each other from month to month. The needs of staff should fuel learning and ultimately help a school achieve its goals. The importance of harnessing the momentum and maintaining focus on what teachers need cannot be overstated.

Billy Joel released a #1 hit song in 1989 called "We Didn't Start the Fire." The truth of the matter is that many principals could join along in this chorus. "We don't start a fire" because we don't focus on any one thing long enough to spark sustainability. We are as guilty as anyone of putting out the flames and passion for learning that our teachers naturally possess. We've dampened their spirits by piling on initiatives and misusing meeting time. A new staff learning paradigm is possible when principals establish focus while leveraging flipped PD.

Champion Learning in Your School

How to champion learning using the flipped approach:
1. Ask your staff what interests them so that flipped PD topics are responsive to staff needs.
2. Keep flipped videos short; five minutes or less usually suffices.
3. Use flipped PD to maximize face-to-face learning time by planning for staff conversation and small-group dialogue.
4. Accept failure as part of the learning process; the first flipped PD experience you plan will be markedly different from the tenth. You *will* get better with practice.

Trying a new approach like flipped PD is tangible evidence that you're committed to learning, but how will you empower others in their learning through flipped PD? The game plan will require a willingness to learn from failure as well as a servant mindset. You have the opportunity to collaborate with your staff on championship-caliber PD that's affirming and has a direct impact on classroom instruction. The payoff will be huge, as long as you are prepared to learn from mistakes that will inevitably be made along the way.

One of the greatest examples of embracing the heart of a champion while making real-time adjustments came from the 1993 NFL Playoffs when the Buffalo Bills were down 35-3 in the third quarter. The Bills went on to score five unanswered touchdowns and pulled off one of the most dramatic comebacks in sports history. The strong finish was made possible by every member of the team rallying together and their willingness to learn while making important in-game adjustments.

These types of in-game adjustments are exactly what is required from principals making the change to flipped meeting formats. The transition will require a dynamic game plan and collaboration with staff. Regardless of whether your PD is currently not-so-good or pretty-darn-good, it can be better! To realize incremental improvements in PD practices, principals must embrace their roles as lead learners.

To foster a reverence for PD and staff learning, a lead learner must ask a few questions. *What do teachers want from their professional development? What do they need? Who should be the one to answer these questions?* I believe that the answer to effective professional development begins and ends with teachers. By valuing their time, we can begin to structure PD in a manner that is responsive to staff needs and not *in spite* of staff needs! When flipping PD, staff learning must be revered. The simple act of flipping is not the goal; instead, it's all about supporting staff learning. We model this by attaching teaching recertification credits to nearly every staff learning experience. This not only honors teachers' time, but it holds us to a high standard in planning meetings. The focus must be learning.

> **Flip-Tip for Admin:** *Start by asking teachers what they need. Create a list of topics staff members are interested in. From there you can identify a single topic that could be best explored through the flipped format. You might even offer two topics so staff members have a choice in their learning!*

If you organize or implement any form of flipped PD that's absent best practice for teaching and learning, you are destined to fail. Flipping a traditional staff meeting without regard to best practice will result in an epic loss. I've seen videos posted online of principals that "flip" meeting content by video-taping 30-50 minute monologues. I don't care how polished your public speaking is, standing face-to-face and presenting information to staff for 30+ minutes in a faculty meeting is a bad idea. Why would the idea be any better on video? If anything, flipped PD videos should be more focused and a catalyst to deeper learning and collaboration. No matter what your approach, it's always about the learning.

There is a tried and true game plan for creating flipped PD videos that leads to deeper learning; the game plan involves clock management. I've found that flipped meeting and flipped PD videos that exceed five minutes in duration lose their impact (and audience) exponentially as time increases. Typically, all a person needs is five minutes to relay important information via video. Ironically, when outside presenters request our staff meeting time to share information they usually request 10-15 minutes. However, when we work with them to create flipped meeting videos, they are able to create five minute presentations that flow rather well. We started flipping meetings to maximize our face-to-face learning time, and the results have been overwhelmingly positive.

There is a positive correlation between a principal's ability to listen and how responsive PD is to teachers' needs. Last year we collected staff feedback on the various PD experiences we facilitated. The feedback was overwhelmingly positive, and served as a testament to the multitude of evolutions our staff meetings and PD experiences have undergone to get us to this point. Our PD team feels like we have a winning game plan for PD because it's built largely on staff needs and feedback. Nevertheless, we're still making in-game adjustments to improve the experience for teachers.

This year we collected feedback about staff PD requests and topics of interest using an online forum entitled, "Flipped PD: Empowered Learning." The title was intentional because we want staff to understand how important their feedback and needs are in the planning of PD. Have you ever completed a survey and felt as if your input did not factor into anything but the recycle bin? It's a demoralizing feeling to be asked for input on decisions that have already been made. Our PD team is comprised of exemplary educators who innately understand the value of feedback. That's why we named the forum in which we collected staff feedback "Empowered Learning."

The term "empowered" signifies a shift in power from principal as PD director to staff as shared stakeholders in learning. The input collected via the "Flipped PD: Empowered Learning" forum will be used to plan PD next school year. Our site data team will reconvene in August to review student achievement data as well as staff requests for PD. The list below includes some of the requests from staff that were submitted via the "Flipped PD: Empowered Learning" forum:

- Genius Hour
- Social Media in Education
- Twitter
- Connecting/Collaborating with Classrooms across the Country
- Math Workshop Model
- Flipped Instruction for students
- Passion Time
- Project Based Learning
- MakerSpaces
- Digital Daily 5 (Integrating Tech. into Literacy Instruction)
- 21st Century Skills
- Inquiry-Based Learning
- Mental Health Training
- Cultural Proficiency
- Going Paperless with 1:1 iPads
- Responsive Classroom
- Technology Integration to Support Student Writing
- Cross-Grade and Department Collaboration

As we begin planning for meaningful staff PD experiences next year, we'll reflect upon what areas align with school goals and then work diligently to plan flipped PD and breakout session options that are responsive to staff needs. We are so committed to staff learning that we are planning to make our site PD breakout sessions and flipped PD optional next school year. We believe our PD should be so professionally affirming that staff would choose it if given the option. We are still collaborating on how this will look, but I'm confident it is the right thing for our Blue Ribbon staff and school. Our ultimate goal is empowered learners who are unswervingly supported in their efforts to make a difference for our students.

Be Inclusive to Hook Everyone

How to include all staff using the flipped approach:
1. Provide technology support and training on the front end if you plan to use blended learning or online forum postings as part of your flipped PD approach. Don't assume all staff have the same background experiences with technology.
2. Reflect upon the value and relevance of flipped and face-to-face PD through different lenses (Ex. general education teachers, Special Education staff, paraprofessionals, and PE/Music departments.) Ask yourself how each of these staff will be honored and included.
3. Use flipped PD and videos as a tool to actively engage more staff and stakeholders with the "vision" and essential learning. Too often PD opportunities are reserved for teachers; using flipped PD can empower other stakeholders in the professional growth process.

One of the primary reasons we flip PD is because every staff member matters. Everyone gets a voice. As principals and lead learners, we need to set the bar highest for ourselves in planning inclusive PD. It's been a couple years since I've seen a teacher correcting papers in a staff meeting, but when this happens the first person I need to confront is me. Effective PD has hooks that support and inspire all staff.

The importance of being inclusive and using "hooks" was modeled for me at a very young age. Some of my fondest memories growing up include fishing with my dad. There was a time that I decided to purchase an artificial "talking frog" lure that was so complicated that I probably spent more time testing the circuit than fishing. My dad always allowed me to make my own decisions when fishing...even when they involved problematic talking lures. My dad probably knew that the lures I selected would be less than productive, but he empowered me to make choices in the lure selection process. My dad's willingness to honor my choice was a powerful "hook" that led to a lifelong love of angling.

My love for fishing and taking risks with different lures was not born from mandates; it was cultivated by a caring dad that included me in the process. I eventually came to understand that the complexity of my talking frog lure was excluding me from the actual fishing experience, and this realization begs an important point: including all staff requires balance between process and content.

When principals plan PD that covers complex or technical material and try to get too fancy with the execution, they may unknowingly exclude some staff. The opposite is also true; traditional PD meetings may lack relevance and not have engaging hooks that are applicable to all staff members. Staff meetings and PD must be inclusive experiences.

I've heard it said that if a professional development activity is "process heavy" the content should be "light." Conversely, if the process is familiar and understandable to all, the content can be a little more involved.

One of my epic leadership failures involved planning a flipped PD session that was process *and* product heavy. I made the mistake of projecting my comfort with online learning onto all of our staff. The specific session was comprised of some deeper work around Culturally Proficient Teaching. I had videos, research, and articles for staff to select from. After interacting with the material, we were to do some online forum postings and respond to one another in conversation threads. The entire experience was modeled after the doctoral classes I had just completed. The only problem was that I had ignored that fact that not everyone had the same background experiences with online and flipped learning as I had.

Many teachers didn't bat an eyelash when it came to this blended approach. Some thrived and their learning was evidenced by in-depth and thought-provoking forum responses. Subsequent meeting conversations were also rich. However, other staff members had basic questions about the flipped PD process that I had failed to address.

Questions ranged from technical steps pertaining to accessing the forum to inquiries about who would be able to view online postings. They were all great questions, and in my excitement to offer a rigorous and reflective staff learning experience, I had failed to proactively address them. I quickly came to realize that PD is for all staff and not solely for those that are technology savvy. Fortunately, I work in a school with exemplary teacher-leaders, and we are able to provide feedback to one another in an honest and caring manner. Based on this feedback, we made some adjustments to be more inclusive of all staff.

We responded by offering more choice and different pathways to expected outcomes. These pathways were inclusive of different staff member's needs. By offering choice, we were adhering to the lessons my dad taught me about inclusion and hooks. We also reclaimed the essential balance between process and content complexity that had been compromised for some staff. The guiding questions and growth to be realized was too important to our students' futures to make the actual content optional, but we did make the process multimodal. Teachers were encouraged to choose between the flipped meeting and online forum postings or a more traditional face-to-face faculty conversation. I participated in both options and found them to be equally engaging.

We also knew that we needed to build staff capacity so that the flipped approach and the use of various technology tools would enhance our learning in the future, rather than be an impediment. We went back to the basics: we practiced online forum responses in Moodle. This was done by asking for staff PD input and requests while everyone was in the same room together. Nothing threatening or complicated...just tell us what you need to be successful. One person suggested that we post comic strips or short cartoons for staff to respond to and practice online posting. The point is, start with content that is easy when you're introducing a process that's different. Flipped PD and forum responses were different for us, and I learned that a principal can't discount the learning required when a process changes.

The importance of inclusion also applies to other staff and stakeholders. For several years, our dedicated paraprofessionals (teaching assistants) have requested to be more involved in our school. Our paraprofessionals want to be part of important building communications. They want to feel valued. We happen to think that our paraprofessionals are amazing and want to include them in PD and staff meetings. We added a paraprofessional to our site PD team, and this person is empowered to help us plan PD for the building. We planned one of our site PD days to honor and include our paraprofessionals. We included them in our end-of-year PLC celebration and staff awards ceremony. Learning is not just for our teachers; it's for everyone, and this message reverberates in our school focus of positive relationships.

Flipping portions of staff meetings can be more inclusive to paraprofessionals and clerical staff as well. One challenge has been that our paraprofessionals' hours vary, and they are not always at school when our staff meetings are scheduled. Recently, I needed to communicate important information about the process for classroom changes and facility use with staff. However, e-mail was not the most effective communication conduit because it can be difficult to discern tone, intent, and care in writing.

To convey these characteristics, I relied on a flipped video podcast that all staff could preview. We then met to do a deeper dive and some collaborative brainstorming around the topic. I included our paraprofessionals in the preliminary podcast so that every person on staff heard the same message. It's human nature to fill in the blanks when information is lacking, and flipping staff meetings addresses this tendency by sharing the same message and narrative directly with all staff.

In the example above, I was able to provide all staff with some important considerations, background information, and guiding principles on classroom usage so they clearly knew my thinking and heart on the issue. Furthermore, the approach was inclusive of all staff (by design). The feedback was positive as well. One staff member even e-mailed me to share, "Thanks, Brad, the video was very easy to understand and was helpful for me to view in advance in this flipped manner." I found that the actual face-to-face meeting with staff was more productive. We spent less time on minutiae involved with classroom usage because that had been conveyed in advance via a succinct (less than five minutes) podcast.

> **Flip-Tip for Admin:** *Flipped PD can enhance connectedness when done effectively. If you have a difficult or sensitive update to provide, be certain you include individual staff that may be impacted using 1:1 conversations first. Otherwise, flipping your meetings is a great way to include everyone in the communication.*

You can see that being inclusive is not only a best practice, but it also ensures that staff learning is an all-hands-on-deck approach. We'd expect nothing less of our students, so why would we compromise on our staff? Look for opportunities to be inclusive of all staff, and carefully monitor the complexity of both PD content and process to ensure a balance is struck. Include all staff by honoring the varying readiness levels around a new topic and the process being used for learning. Inclusive leadership involves effective communication, differentiation, and a servant-heart. Involve your people and they will be more equipped to make a difference for kids.

Purpose Drives Practice

How to be purposeful when planning flipped PD:
1. When planning any PD experience, identify the purpose *first* and then determine the process.
2. If you decide to flip a PD experience, be sure to explicitly communicate the purpose. Share this purpose when conversing with individuals, at staff meetings, and within any flipped PD videos you're creating.
3. Be certain that the purpose you've identified supports staff learning and honors their time.

Purposeful leaders serve their staff by collaborating on the creation of a shared vision and the pragmatic means of attaining it.

We live in an era of perpetual change, and our schools are relying on principals and lead learners to navigate the change in a purposeful manner. Former U.S. Army Chief of Staff General Eric Shinseki said, "If you don't like change, you're going to like irrelevance even less." I don't know many teachers that are opposed to purposeful change; it's when change seems arbitrary or overwhelming that principals encounter resistance. Purposeful PD must drive practice.

As I reflect upon my purpose as a principal, I often think about what I consider to be one of the greatest inventions of my lifetime. My Global Positioning System (GPS) has helped me arrive at my destination more times than I care to admit. I love hearing my GPS proclaim, "You are now at your destination." It's blissful! There are also times when my GPS adjusts course due to road construction. In these instances, I hear my GPS inform me, "Rerouting." After this announcement, we're back on track. My GPS is constantly monitoring my route and rerouting based on my proximity to a destination. The purpose of my GPS is unmistakable, and it has delivered me to my destination successfully countless times.

Principals must constantly monitor the purpose for staff meetings and PD. We would never decide what road to travel before identifying our destination. Why do we often gravitate to traditional PD formats regardless of purpose? In a similar vein, it doesn't make any sense to hop in a car and drive around aimlessly without a purpose. However, how many times have staff meetings meandered purposelessly, much to the chagrin of our dedicated teachers? My advice is to always, *always* start by identifying the purpose first, and then plan the process, content, directions, etc. from there.

A couple years ago, our staff meetings were somewhat disjointed and lacked coherence from month to month. Meeting topics were dictated by external requests for our time. There were many talented educators and administrators in the district, and they all wanted a slice of our staff meeting time to present information. We realized that we needed to prioritize our professional learning over some of these updates, so flipping the traditional manner in which information was shared seemed like a logical starting point.
Requests for our meeting time included topics such as the occasional grant opportunity presentation, high-stakes standardized test training, English Learner program updates, math curriculum review communications, budget updates, district recycling information, revisiting literacy initiatives, peer coaching conversations, and

technology. You can see from this list that each of these things is important. Our challenge became how to manage our time so that we were connected to district initiatives and still moving forward on our school improvement goals and professional learning.

There were months when requests by outside presenters actually surpassed the actual number of meeting minutes we had scheduled as a staff. In other words, the time that people wanted to stop by our staff meetings and share with us, actually exceeded the duration of our staff meetings! There was little time for collaboration or PD, and something needed to give. We tried scheduling additional meetings, but *more* of a mediocre thing is not a best practice. Adding more meetings and minutes was not the answer. As principal, I had allowed our staff meetings to go on autopilot without regard to any particular purpose. "Rerouting" was our solution!

Flipping portions of our meetings and these informational presentations was a key part of the shift, and this helped us reclaim our purpose. The purpose for our initial foray into flipped staff meetings was clear; we wanted to protect our time together as a staff to increase our ability to collaborate and learn about topics that directly related to shared school goals. This is when our amazing PD team put our staff learning into overdrive. They helped us get back on track and navigate decisions about PD meetings with purpose in mind.

I began having conversations with the district staff and outside presenters that were interested in dropping in on our next staff meeting for "just 10 or 15 minutes." The conversations shifted from what date might work for them to stop by and present, to what the purpose of their proposed visits were. This served as a springboard to conversation about other forms of communication.

We began to leverage technology and Web 2.0 tools to create win-win scenarios. One of our primary means of changing the training and communication paradigm was through video podcasting. Initially, I sensed a reluctance to shift to digital tools to communicate with our staff. One obstacle was that the presenters requesting time at our meetings were not always comfortable or proficient with the production tools needed to create video podcasts. Our solution was to offer that technical support along with the invitation to create the podcasts with them. Another obstacle was that the flipped staff meeting approach was different than anyone had experienced at the time.

Over the course of several months, we found that flipped video podcasting presentations required less camera-time than the in-person meeting time that had originally been requested. Their video podcasts were more succinct and on point. This saved our staff valuable time.

We communicated the purpose of the flipped staff meetings to faculty, so they understood that we were ultimately honoring their time while shifting our face-to-face meetings to purposeful learning time. We still hold a monthly check-in meeting with staff to discuss important school issues, but this is coupled with monthly PD breakout session choices facilitated by staff.

> **Flip-Tip for Admin:* Be prepared to respond to teachers when they ask how flipping PD or meetings really saves them time. Be sure you are not just adding extra videos/research for them to complete outside the school day. Your purpose will include deeper staff learning, but an underlying purpose should be honoring staff time. Try cancelling or condensing a regularly-scheduled meeting to drive home the support.*

Without the introduction of flipped meeting content, we would not have been able to realize this transition. The impact has been astonishing, and most staff members look forward to making choices about their learning at these breakout PD sessions. Moving forward, we are planning to further support staff by flipping additional breakout PD experiences next year. As a result, staff interested in deeper learning or applying for recertification credits will be empowered with additional options.

We will accomplish this next iteration by asking PD breakout session presenters to offer flipped content (research, videos, forum interactions) prior to each face-to-face breakout session. This will serve two purposes; it will maximize the face-time when teachers are learning together, and it will fulfill some state requirements making it more convenient for teachers to earn recertification credits.

Purpose continues to drive our PD planning and every iteration is intended to further empower staff learning and support the teachers that make a difference for kids every single day. To reiterate, we do not flip all of our staff meetings, and we are very intentional about what content is flipped.

Possible Flipped PD Purposes:
1. Flip a staff meeting to *model* the flipped approach for teachers. Reflect upon the pedagogy and potential impact on student learning.
2. Flip components of a staff meeting or training to *honor teachers' time* and make the learning more convenient and accessible.
3. Flip a meeting or announcement in which you want everyone to hear a *consistent message*. A video podcast is conducive to sharing with an entire staff regardless of varying schedules.
4. Flip random outside presentations to *protect professional development time*.
5. Flip PD to *go deeper* into an area of study or to *build background information* prior to a face-to-face PD experience.
6. Flip PD to *provide recertification or continuing education units* (CEUs) for staff.
7. Flip PD to *maximize face-time together*. Staff meetings should not be one-sided information dissemination...that's called e-mail.

We also learned that sometimes the purpose of a meeting may be multi-faceted. For example, an introductory meeting about peer coaching might be scheduled to convey basic information about peer coaching, but personally connecting with staff to begin to build trust and relationships might also be a goal. This is why identifying the purpose for a PD experience is pivotal.

A Call to Arms: The Time is Now
The path to purposeful PD requires an unswerving focus on learning. The learning must be "for all staff" and not "done to staff." Lead with a servant-heart and be responsive to the needs of teachers who are in the trenches each and every day. They are the all-stars who are ultimately responsible for championing student learning in our classrooms. Always remember that a diverse staff (grade-levels,

content areas, experience levels, etc.) will have varying backgrounds and professional needs. Rest assured, when your staff is ready to begin flipping PD, mid-game adjustments will be necessary, but the rewards outweigh the risks. Their learning matters and our students are counting on us to model what it means to be empowered learners in a digital age. There is no time like the present to make a difference for students and staff; it's their time to shine!

Dr. Brad Gustafson is an elementary principal in Minnesota. An innovative administrator, Brad has pioneered efforts to transform pedagogy to reflect best practices in a digital age. He is committed to leveraging technology as a transformative tool that inspires creativity, connectivity, and innovation. Brad is a TEDx and keynote speaker, and exudes a passion for leadership that is palpable.

Brad is a TouchCast Ambassador and received the Best EduCast Award in 2014 from TouchCast. His podcast, the #30SecondTake, is featured on the Education Podcasting Network and engages thought-leaders in focused conversations pertaining to critical issues in education. When he's not podcasting he can be found blogging about leadership, learning, and technology.

Brad's blog, Adjusting Course, was recognized with an Editor's Choice Content Award in 2015 by Smartbrief Education. It was named as a "Must-Read" K-12 blog by EdTech Magazine. The blog was recognized as a finalist for Best Administrator Blog by the EduBlog Awards the past two years. Brad was an Academy of Education Arts and Sciences Bammy Award Nominee in the category of Elementary School Principal the past two years as well. In 2014 he was the national Digital Innovation in Learning Honorable Mention from EdSurge and Digital Promise.

Brad earned his Doctoral degree at Bethel University where his research focused on leading innovative professional development.

Twitter: @GustafsonBrad
Website: adjustingcourse.wordpress.com

What is Voxer?

Dr. Joe Mazza

Voxer has become extremely popular in the education space, perhaps because the Personal Learning Network, or PLN, has evolved over the years. The "network" has grown up a bit since many K-12 organizations embraced the research stating that social networking circles are more than a passing fad.

"Voxing" is when you use the free mobile app called Voxer to participate in an asynchronous walkie-talkie-like conversation, only it's more like a group text on your phone. You can easily start a conversation with multiple friends and colleagues, or just one. The conversation is chronological, archived inside the app, and allows you to use your voice, send pics, and text where you choose. I started voxing with nine other educational leaders made up of elementary, middle, and high school principals, and superintendents around the country. We began a powerful online conversation through our cell phones using the Voxer app.

With just two clicks on my phone, I quickly enter a virtual world full of inspiring human beings working really hard for kids, teachers, and families. Using Voxer has helped us complement messages sent using Twitter (which has a 140 character limit).

I've spent a lot of time on Twitter over the last 3+ years developing a personal learning network, and as I look across my timeline today, many of those profile pictures are much more than images that share resources; these people are friends, colleagues, and folks I have built real relationships with. Truthfully, I consider my PLN an extension of my staff and my family.

I find myself sending more and more Voxer messages to my close knit PLN. Being able to use my own words (beyond 140 characters) and hear the tone, empathy, and extended articulation in the voices of others around the world helps me connect on a deeper level. The best part is that I can participate whenever it is convenient for me, but can always go back and hear what I missed.

In only one month, our Voxer group has discussed 1:1, blended learning, school assemblies, homework, science fairs, cursive, discipline issues, graduation requirements, common core, teacher/leader burnout, social media to engage families and the community, and probably 50 other areas of our daily work with students, staff and families. Voxing with those in your PLN is like creating your own personal podcast where you can decide in real-time who is involved, when you listen and respond, and what topics you cover.

This thought process, along with other work, has led to the birth of a new #eduvoxers hashtag and Twitter handle (@eduvoxers) that aims to support educators looking to "backchannel" their conversations asynchronously around curriculum, pedagogy, BYOD, family and community engagement, edcamps, and many other topics that educational leaders face in today's field. Check it out here via gettingsmart.com: bit.ly/personalizedpd07

At the following link, you can listen to a ten minute vox from some of my colleagues around the country on how they are using Voxer in their own learning organizations as teachers, school principals, and superintendents (bit.ly/personalizedpd09).

I do most of my voxing safely in the car on my morning and afternoon commutes. I can see a lot of potential for school leadership teams, grade-level teams, HSA-PTA-PTO teams and other educators trying to collaborate on a given topic while striving to respect everyone's busy schedules.

What if your principal provided you a verbal "vox" when walking out of your classrooms in lieu of waiting until the feedback form was provided to you. That verbal tone might mean a great deal to a teacher looking for immediate feedback from his or her lesson. Our #PTchat team of moderators now "vox" during the week to discuss the upcoming chat and ideas for future chats. I now use Voxer with my wife during the day, and other family members as it's just nice to cut down on texting and hear the actual voice of those I care about.

I hope you'll join the extended conversation on Voxer. When you do, please add your name to the growing #eduvoxers Google Doc found here: bit.ly/personalizedpd10.

*Special thanks to the original Voxer group of PLN pals who got me started on Voxer: Tom Whitford, Aaron Becker, Ben Gilpin, Jeff Zoul, Jimmy Casas, Joe Sanfelippo, Tom Murray, Curt Rees & Tony Sinanis.

Dr. Joe Mazza *serves as the Leadership Innovation Manager at the University of Pennsylvania's Graduate School of Education working with Mid-Career Doctoral Program in Educational Leadership (@MCDPEL) and supports the Penn Center for Educational Leadership (PCEL). In the program, he teaches the Digital Leadership module, as well as meets faculty, students, and alumni "where they are" regarding innovative teaching, learning, and leadership. Dr. Mazza serves as a national family-community engagement advisor to the Institute for Educational Leadership in Washington, DC.*

Before transitioning to PennGSE, he served as K-12 Project Manager for Connected Teaching, Learning & Leadership in the North Penn School District in Lansdale PA. Dr. Mazza served as "lead learner" at Knapp Elementary School since 2007 before taking on the district edtech role. He has spent his career working with students, teachers & families as a 3rd grade teacher, bilingual assistant principal, middle school vice-principal, an elementary principal, while serving as a TV studio producer, webmaster and technology integration coach in each setting. Mazza's dissertation topic: The Use of Social Media by School Principals to Communicate Between Home and School.

Twitter: @Joe_Mazza
Websites: leadlearner.com
midcareer.gse.upenn.edu/innovationslab

The Technology You Need
for Flipped PD
Ben Wilkoff

I have been lucky enough to write my own job description...twice.

I say lucky, but you could easily substitute lucky with crazy, and it would be just as true. The first time, I had no idea what I was doing. I wrote out a list of things I wanted to do, and somehow I convinced someone to let me do them while simultaneously getting paid.

The second time, I didn't mess around. I didn't write a job description that anyone could fulfil. I wrote one that was just for me. It had my specific skill-set as requirements. It made real the projects I had been incubating in my blog posts and podcasts for years. You see, writing your role into existence means that you can't rely on precedent. Any expectations that exist are your own. And then you start the work, it becomes ever more clear that you will learn more every day about what it is you do.

The work, as it turns out, is enormous. The role I defined for myself is in the service of nearly 6000 teachers, 90,000 students, and across over 180 schools. In the face of such an immense scope, I needed to find something to tether myself to: a set of essential truths that would keep me afloat as I continued to find the right impact points. While this may not be representative of your exact institution, it is my sincere hope that these goals are reflected in your own work. You see, these are the ones that have helped me define my role and to keep moving toward our district vision of "Every Child Succeeds."

- Teachers and Leaders should be connected to each other. Isolated classrooms and schools are the enemy of innovation.

- Teachers and Leaders should personalize their own professional learning based upon their strengths, needs, interests, and constraints.

- Self-reflection is the key to change.

These factors tend to drive the way PD can take place within our district. They help to define the ways in which teachers and leaders can own their professional learning, flipping the PD in the process. It is in these three important factors that I have staked my claim as the Director of Personalized Professional Learning in Denver Public Schools, and they are the same ones that I would like to explore here.

Eliminating Isolated Classrooms

Every classroom is set up to be self-contained, or more accurately, isolated. The teacher is set up to be self-sufficient, to instruct her students without interference from the rest of the world. In many ways, each classroom is its own one-room schoolhouse. From the finite resources that are stored in the classroom to the expectations on students to work independently, dozens of these one-room schoolhouses are found within each school building.

In my work with teachers, it is this mentality of the one-room schoolhouse that I have to combat more than any other. Teachers question whether or not they should be sharing their lesson plans, opening their classroom doors, or worrying about the other "schoolhouses" down the hall when they have just about all they can handle within their own.

Google+ Communities: (bit.ly/personalizedpd12) I have found no other social network that is specifically engineered toward a community perspective. There are hundreds of specific content area communities, but the power of this network is when you get together with other educators and discuss your practice on a daily basis. It is the "coming back" to a community that creates relationships.

<u>Using G+ Communities to eliminate isolated classrooms</u>: Sharing your classroom, specifically what kinds of work you are doing within your classroom, can be a huge undertaking if you are trying to do so all from a central and isolated website. While this works for some people, many people have a lot of different interests and the work that they do cannot be easily fit into a single "bucket" of a blog or wiki. Rather, it works much better to join multiple different communities of practice on Google+ in order to engage in the specific (and different) conversations that you are passionate about. By joining the 42 communities I take part in (bit.ly/personalizedpd14), I am able to engage fully in each conversation about "Google Apps" or "English Language Acquisition" with a group of passionate educators that want to do the same.

Google Photo Spheres and **ThingLink.com** - (bit.ly/personalizedpd16) Sharing a single image of your classroom is one thing, but being able to share a 360 degree view or an annotated perspective of your classroom is quite different. Google Photo Spheres allow you to capture everything going on within your classroom during a single moment and later explore them on your computer or mobile device. ThingLink lets you take a picture and then create "hot spots" on top of the image that link to more information or rich media.

<u>Using it to eliminate isolated classrooms</u>: By capturing your classroom in its entirety and/or providing additional context for it with media and links, you are able to quite literally show your hard work to other teachers who can appreciate it and, in turn, share their own. It is in this back-and-forth between teachers that new ideas get shared and innovative practices can take hold.

Mozilla's Popcorn.webmaker.org and **Touchcast.com** - While ThingLink is great for annotating and providing context upon images, Popcorn and Touchcast are for doing the same thing with video. While this may not seem revolutionary, the ability to place ideas on top of video or provide links to further explore content allows for deep analysis of teaching practice videos or specific annotations of content-heavy topics that would otherwise whiz right by the viewer.

> Utilizing it to eliminate isolated classrooms:
> Whenever a teacher captures their classroom through video, there are always things that are left behind. For example, you can't really see what the students are working on at their seats. You also can't really know what the teacher was using to present from on her computer. By annotating these videos using Popcorn or Touchcast, you can add all of those pieces of context that are so necessary for digging in to a teacher's practice.

VideoNot.es - Taking notes while watching a video can be maddening. Especially as you are having to start and stop the video a whole bunch of times just so you know what timestamp related to which idea. With Video Not.es, your notes are automatically synced to the video.

> Using it to eliminate isolated classrooms:
> Watching yourself teach on video is one of the most nerve-wracking things you can do, and yet it is one of the most effective as well. However, sharing that video and having someone else provide feedback is pretty difficult without a way to sync up those two "viewings." Video Not.es eliminates the isolation of having to watch and reflect alone. Because you can share your own notes with others and have them contribute to them as well, it is like you can have an asynchronous viewing party for your classroom. It is the ideal way to conduct learning labs in a virtual setting.

Video Hangouts or Skype.com – (bit.ly/personalizedpd18) Staying Connected with other classrooms and schools around you has never been easier, and these two tools really take any lingering difficulty out of the equation. The fact that you can now have up to 15 people on the same video call (in a Google Apps for Education account), means that you can screenshare or conduct a rigorous panel discussion any time you have a computer or mobile device handy.

> Using it to eliminate isolated classrooms:
> When you are able to see and discuss your own teaching struggles and triumphs with other teachers and not just

rely upon the text communication of a forum or blog post, you are really able to see the value of the relationship you are building as a part of the professional learning experience. Video conferencing opens up the walls of the classroom to visit museums (bit.ly/personalizedpd20) or fellow classrooms around the world (bit.ly/personalizedpd22).

When I ventured into one such singular "schoolhouse" in a science classroom within our district, I was met with a young teacher who was daily trying to engage students through small group lessons and lab experiments. Her frenetic pace throughout the lesson I observed spoke to the fact that she was the only one she knew who was trying these lessons in this way. She believed herself an island, differentiating and scaffolding to students without any hope of the same for her own professional learning.

It isn't that she didn't want to collaborate or to learn from others, though. It is just that we, as a system, haven't set up the structures and the incentives to do so. Many teachers and leaders simply don't know what collaboration looks like, and how they would go about it if they were given the opportunity.

This is a central focus for PD: modeling collaboration. In every structure, in every event, we should be modeling the types of collaboration that break down the walls of the one-room schoolhouse. We should be starting conversations that do not end when the "bell rings" and they leave the PD. But what does this look like?

I believe it looks like an Online Community of Practice. And more than that, it looks like intentionally leading teachers through why they would want a community in the first place.

Whenever I lead a new group of teachers and leaders through the creation of an online community, I ask them three questions:

1. What makes a group a community?
2. What makes a community into a community of practice?
3. Why should we put that community online?

It is through the answering of those three questions that educators understand the potential of online communities. It is through talking to one another about what they want out of the rest of the group, about their expectations for one another that they finally come to an understanding of why they need to break down the walls and to contribute to one another's teaching in an authentic way.

Google+ - (plus.google.com) By far, one of the easiest ways to create community amongst adults. Because everyone has to "be themselves" within Google+, there is a lot that you can do to start building a portfolio of posts and ideas that are tied to real teachers and leaders. The communities functionality combined with Video Hangouts are a powerful twosome. This means you can not only have ongoing conversations, but you can meet people face-to-face whenever you need to pull folks together to discuss something.

    <u>Great Use Cases</u>:
    ◊ Online communities of Practice
    ◊ Extended discussions on important educational topics.
    ◊ Connecting with great educators locally and beyond

Cel.ly - SMS is a highly underrated tool in the classroom. By utilizing texting with teachers and learners, you are leveraging the device that they have with them at all times. You can start discussions in simple ways or make it easier for folks to share their ideas in an informal manner. By maintaining a "group" SMS chat, you are ensuring that all of the ideas are instantaneous and captured for later reflection.

    <u>Great Use Cases</u>:
    ◊ Group dialogues on a particular article
    ◊ Educational "chats" in a private group
    ◊ Organizing events or sessions using a simple text
    message

Google Docs – (docs.google.com) At this point, it might not be worth mentioning, but using Google Docs for collaboration within Professional Learning is almost a given at this point. The ability to collaborate with up to 50 participants at the same time (or over time, if you need to do so asynchronously) cannot be overstated. Collaboration is key to engagement, and Google Docs is the easiest tool for ensuring this happens.

Great Use Cases:
◊ A collaborative notes document
◊ A collaborative brainstorming document for new or promising teaching practices
◊ A way to ensure next steps are claimed and followed up
◊ A learning log or professional development plan

Building community starts slowly. The first question is about getting those first few hands in the air. It is about taking what they already know about groups they are in and getting them to think about what binds them together. The second question is getting each of them to process what about their practice they are willing to share. It is considering what opening the door to their classroom actually looks like for them. The third question is about getting them to understand what is truly unique about this time period for teaching. It is looking at what is possible now that wasn't previously. Once they have that understanding, they are ready to come together and start asking questions of one another, sharing resources with one another, and generally being learners with one another.

It is that third question, about why we should be putting these communities "online", that we get to the heart of why Flipped PD is so powerful. As you can see in the video facilitation of these questions in the following link (bit.ly/personalizedpd23), we focused on the concepts of shifting time, space, and our assumptions for what the confines of a community of practice actually are. But it is the way in which we focus on these concepts that matters. By using a Google Document as our organizing structure, we see the initial modeling of what communities can do together. By using an embedded animation (a Gif) of a Prezi presentation, the key points can be emphasized consistently and within the right order/structure. And, by allowing for extensive commenting we can see what it means when asynchronous opportunities for learning are leveraged. These tools provide the backdrop for the conversation, but the conversation itself is still paramount.

Because it isn't enough that we share lesson plans on Google+ or Twitter. It isn't enough that we make collaborative documents in Google Docs to create interventions for our shared students. The subtle underlying question that we should be asking at any PD event is, Will the group that has assembled today ever become a community? If the answer is no, then we have wasted the event. Modern PD isn't about singular pieces of discrete knowledge. It isn't about perpetuating a system of teacher certificates or seat time. It is about putting together into a cohesive whole all of the learning about reading strategies, technology integration, Understanding by Design, language learner scaffolding, rigorous tasks, learning styles, and any other new initiative your school district is pursuing. Isolated events are never going to bring about the type of change the teachers seek or the districts and schools want. It is only through an ongoing community that we have the type of support we need to truly innovate.

Twitter – (twitter.com) Again, this tool seems like an essential part of the toolkit at this point. It is the way in which educators connect most easily to one another. It is the way in which we share resources and ask questions at all times of the day. It is also the way in which we share our learning "in the moment."

> Great Use Cases:
> ◊ Educational Chats (conducted weekly at specific times and with specific topics)
> ◊ Resource sharing (lots and lots of links)
> ◊ Starting discussion/debate that can be continued elsewhere (Google Docs, Blog posts, phone calls, etc.)

Hangouts Messages – (google.com/hangouts) I have found that having a core group to "hangout" with is an essential component of how I continue to build and test new ideas. By having a few ongoing "chats", I can quickly ask questions about how to handle specific situations with teachers or if I am stuck on a piece of technology that is giving me trouble. These conversations end up being the backbone of any new initiative I try because they provide instant feedback and a supportive ear. The fact that they are private also makes it so I can ask questions or propose ideas that are still too fragile for Twitter.

> Great Use Cases:
> ◊ Ongoing conversations with colleagues (local or global)
> ◊ Office hours
> ◊ Quick Q&A sessions with a mentor/mentee

And what does that innovation look like? It looks like conversations that happen between the one-room schoolhouses in your building. It looks like honest and open dialogue about your practice. In our initial sessions on Communities of Practice, we look at many different examples of these conversations as models. This is one of my favorites from a Google+ post:

Susann Fruendt 3 Feb 2014
FYI, I have a French colleague who taught an English class with me. There were a few problems....

 Marco Pugliesi 3 Feb 2014
I'm a simple English learner but however really passionate on it and I like spending my spare time on it. I knew lot of English in a normal course where I live and other ones here in Google+ , and what that I prefer is who leaves the student speaking freely without remarking each mistakes each time that they make one or more than one.
In my opinion it is a good teacher who teachs with fun , making have fun their students , teaching especially grammar rules maybe through a word game or similar stuff. These are the best methods to study in general but mostly for learning a language.
Obviously the teacher is a teacher and the student always remains a student but if they create a friendly spirit together I believe that satisfaction will be greater for both of them.
For all the reasons I wrote above it's normal that one teacher cannot know every single words (even he/she is a native) and that even he/she can make sometimes some mistakes , no-one is perfect and then you can imagine how boring it would be a lesson together a perfect Teacher and perfect student !!!!

 Susann Fruendt 3 Feb 2014 +1
The case I was talking about was a teacher who seemingly didn't know any more words than his students. He spent a third of the time in class looking up words. In the end, the students revolted and he had to give up the class. Nevertheless, some other colleagues say that his vocabulary wasn't a problem. I agree that it wasn't his only problem, but I find when a teacher uses a text in class (which he chose), he should either know every word or look it up beforehand.
Same thing: if you're going to talk about cars, you should look up related vocabulary (fender, hood, clutch, etc.) before - if you don't know it.

 Blanca Julia Garza Araujo 3 Feb 2014 +1
I have been teaching for a very long time and it has always been my belief that a teacher should anticipate and be prepared. I agree wholeheartedly with Susann Fruendt about looking up related vocabulary of whatever it is you will be teaching. I think students do get tired if a teacher who does not know enough vocabulary. These makes students lose respect in their teacher. I also believe in empowering the student and letting him/her find out the meaning and teach it to the rest of the class, but sometimes the meaning is needed right away and students are not up to looking for the word, or don't have a dictionary at hand, unfortunately. So, in my case, I would definitely be prepared, that also shows the students you care and you are qualified to teach the course. =)

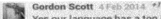

Gordon Scott 4 Feb 2014
Yes our language has a ton of words, and surely I don't know them all. The teacher in question is very unprepared and the students rightly revolted. A knowledgeable person would at least have an idea of a words root and use logic to assess its likely genre and meaning.

Natalie Nel 4 Feb 2014
I agree with Gordon to a point. I find that at times I get stumped between American and British words. There are some words which are so foreign to me and I have to admit to not knowing them. Just the other day, I had to think very hard at the meaning of 'blacktop' as the context it was used in was not something I was familiar with. I then had to ask questions to get the meaning. In the UK and other parts of the world, we use tarmac or road surface.

Jenny Scott 4 Feb 2014
Very much of the opinion that while the teacher is there to provide this kind of help, it's the students who need to be able to find the meanings. I give them the dictionary resources to be able to find the meanings themselves.

Susann Fruendt 4 Feb 2014
I'm not saying that a teacher should serve as a dictionary and simply translate every word every time somebody asks him. I do, however, think that a teacher should know the words in his own material.
Many of you say to let students look up words themselves – I'm not a big fan of this. (It might be important to add that I teach adults who know how to use a dictionary.) I prefer to have students explain the word in English rather than blurt out a translation, because when you or another student explain the word, they will really understand it and it will help them to remember the word.
Instead of people quietly looking up all kinds of words, I also prefer them to ask out loud because if they don't know it, there is probably someone else who doesn't either. It also gives me an idea of how difficult the text/exercise is for the class.

Notice the diversity of support and opinion. Notice the back-and-forth of ideas. More than anything, though, notice the community. These are teachers that are coming together with a shared purpose to help one another be better. This is the kind of PD that sticks. This is the kind of PD that connects us all together. And it should be the norm, and not the exception.

Personalized Professional Learning
No two teachers have the same exact need, and yet we build PD as if they do. No two teachers have the same strengths, and yet we pick an ability level for a session or course, and we do not waiver from it. The diversity of experience found amongst teachers has led to many different interests and capacities for change and growth. No two teachers are alike. The sooner we come around to developing them that way, the closer we will be to serving them fully.

So, how do we see these teachers more clearly? How do we build support for the whole teacher and not just the subset that we want to develop?

It starts by telling the whole story of what it means to be a teacher. Traditionally, we have seen teachers as only that figurehead that is standing in front of the classroom, rather than a human being with responsibilities and aspirations outside of the 8-4 school day. She is not a martyr, and she is not a saint. The teacher is human, fallible, and amazing. She is the one who will pull gains in a student from nothing, and she is the same one who will be too tired from getting up with her 3-month-old the night before to fully execute her lesson plan. It is the complexity that we must see, first and foremost.

Personalized PD is about starting any type of support for teachers with identifying the four core areas of a Professional Learning Profile: Strengths, Needs, Interests, and Constraints. It is only after fully fleshing out this profile that you can see the whole teacher, and then truly support her with PD.

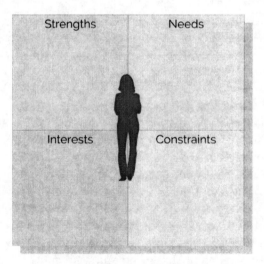

By knowing her profile, which is different from every other teacher-leader, you can start to flip the professional learning according to what has been identified. For example, if a teacher's strength happens to be content-area expertise but a need is in technological understanding, the flipping strategy would be much more around mentoring the teacher through tech tools that assume an advanced knowledge of the standards.

While this profile is important to identify, it is even more important to show that it is not static. It is also not a personality test or entirely subjective. Rather, this profile should be developed in conjunction with data from observation and feedback as well as self-reflection. The following sections will go into each facet of the Personalized Professional Learning profile. While the tools for capitalizing on this profile are explained throughout these sections, it is important to call out several of them from the beginning:

Tools for supporting professional learning according to Strengths, Needs, Interests, and Constraints:

Google Forms/Spreadsheets - An essential component of how you can capture data and analyze it in real time (google.com/forms).

Autocrat - A Google Spreadsheet Add-on that allows for sophisticated mail-merging of data submitted through a form (bit.ly/personalizedpd24).

Google+ Hangouts on Air - The ability to record video conferences (to Youtube) for later use (plus.google.com/hangouts/onair).

Explain Everything - A screencasting app for iOS that allows for sophisticated flipped lessons (bit.ly/personalizedpd26).

Google Drive - The hub for every type of collaborative tool/file type you need for PD (google.com/drive).

Twitter - The largest Professional Learning Network tool for educators (twitter.com).

Skype - Cross-platform Video and Audio conferencing (skype.com).

Google Groups - An email group that allows for collaborative tasking and daily digests of content (groups.google.com).

Strengths:
We tend not to care what a teacher is good at already in PD. In fact, most of the time we just forget that they have any expertise at all. We are working on their weaknesses. We don't have time to bring their strengths into the equation.

There is a huge flaw in this logic. It assumes that we, as professional developers, are the holders of all knowledge. It depends upon the facility that we know what great teaching looks like, and that those that are in the classroom do not. Any time I find myself in this mindset, I have to repeat my own personal mantra for Flipped PD: We are not the only experts in the room.

In any room of teachers, the sheer number of years of expertise is overwhelming. The depth of experience is so vast that to not rely on it is criminal. If we deny the strengths of each of the teachers before us, we are denying their ability to take what they know and apply it to something new. We are disallowing their ability to become a community of teachers and learners. We are cutting them off from the part of themselves that is most competent in favor of the part that feels most weak. This cannot happen.

Like the time I trusted that another teacher could explain better than I could why Explain Everything was the right app for screencasting on the iPad. She went through and showed just how you could construct a lesson that started with an essential question and then continue to zoom in as the topic grew most specific.

Or the time when a teacher-leader spoke up and identified how she was organizing documents in her Google Drive to ensure all of her team members could have access to them and collaborate on a moment's notice.

This isn't me abdicating my responsibilities as a Professional Developer. It is me assuming the role of Lead Learner, modeling the ways we honor the experiences and expertise that surround us.

Google Moderator - This tool allows you to collect a whole bunch of different ideas from a group of people (no matter how large) and it lets them evaluate their relative merit through voting. This makes it very easy for great ideas, questions, or suggestions to raise to the top (google.com/moderator).
> Great Use Cases:
> ◊ Brainstorming lesson ideas for the classroom
> ◊ Generating debate topics for students.
> ◊ Creating an ongoing list of project ideas

The Post-it Plus App - This tool is all about going from the physical generation of ideas to the digital application of those ideas. This app lets you take a picture of a set of post-it notes and then digitally manipulate each one (bit.ly/personalizedpd28).

Great Use Cases:
◊ Capturing a great design thinking session
◊ Allowing for students to manipulate ideas on stickies into unique groupings

Padlet.com - A digital corkboard application that doubles as a well-designed collaborative posting platform. Padlet is incredibly versatile and is beautiful as well. I highly recommend it for making digital sticky notes with images and links embedded.

Great Use Cases:
◊ A vision board for a big project
◊ Digital brainstorming and idea sharing

Needs:

This is the one that we tend to focus on most, but we have such a narrow definition of need that is squeezes out the actual teacher in the process. Most of the time we define "the need" as the outcome that the teacher is trying to achieve. Whether it is in writing a better Student Learning Objective or in doing better student data analysis, the need we identify is typically generic and sterile. The needs we see can apply to a vast array of teachers, rather than any one teacher in particular. We have to stop doing this.

When asked, the needs that most teachers identify are specific to their own classrooms. They are even specific to the kids that are in front of them this year. This is not a failure to see the big picture. This is the big picture. These kids are the ones that are important, right now.

So let's find solutions for them. Let's build PD that helps them to learn better. Let's listen to the problems that are being encountered in the classroom and not to a fictionalized version of them that we have created as an amalgam of all the teachers we have worked with.

A fourth grade teacher wanted to know how classroom management should change now that she had a center set of Chromebooks in her classroom. She didn't want to know how you should ideally use those chromebooks, she wanted a system that would allow her students to thrive in the face of this new opportunity. She wanted to talk to another teacher who had been there.

So, that is what we did. Connecting the two of them on Twitter and then later on Skype.

The 8th grade language arts teacher who wanted a better way to assess writing wasn't asking for better writing prompts or a better rubric. Fundamentally, he was asking for a more authentic audience for his kids. He wanted an opportunity for those in the community to look at student essays and to provide feedback. He wanted an avenue to better writing that didn't include a red pen.

So, that is what we did. Introducing him to Quadblogging across schools. He found his audience, both locally and around the world. We could have done this with the flat classroom project or Comments4Kids, but all we really needed was to start somewhere.

It was in listening to these teachers, in identifying real needs rather than perceived needs that we were able to support the whole teacher. It is much more like prescribing a custom treatment than just putting them on an antibiotic to cure anything that ails you.

Interests:
We typically ignore these in designing PD for teachers. As an educator, your interests may lie outside of the discipline you are paid to teach. Or, they may present a unique approach for tackling your given subject. It is these interests, though, that make up the passion projects from your classroom. They are the core of your engagement.

As a part of a yearlong collaboration with an elementary teacher, I was able to tackle a great many of these passion projects. One such project was when she wanted to find a better way to make a certificate for his/her students. She was not (generally speaking) interested in a spreadsheet that captures student information accurately. And yet, when I showed her an easy way to support the creation of these certificates using a Google Form and Spreadsheet and automatically mail merge to the certificate using Autocrat, she couldn't get enough of playing with the formatting and presentation of the data. It was only when I met the teacher at her interest level, I was then able to find her the tools to help her achieve her PD goals.

Likewise, I was assisting an AP Calculus teacher that wanted to know how to increase his use of Project-Based Learning in a regimented curriculum. He was not specifically interested in writing better assessment questions, so when I introduced him to another math teacher from the other end of the district in a video conference using Google+ Hangouts. They immediately started to compare how their assessment questions were having an effect on the ways groups were forming and the work was in their classrooms. It was when they could see each other, sitting across from a virtual table after fiddling with their webcams for fifteen minutes each, that they were able to make this collaboration happen.

It is by engaging these interests that you find your path to the content that is necessary. The solutions only present themselves when you consider what the teacher actually wants.

Constraints:
We almost never consider the teachers ability to engage as a factor for how much they can learn or change. We don't consider what is going on at home or the many other responsibilities that they have during the school day. This is a mistake.

Teachers capacities for change are immense, but they are not infinite. Defining the barriers to entry is just as important as providing the resources to overcome them. I find this process of identifying these capacity issues to be incredibly freeing for both the teachers I serve and for me as someone who needs to be able to invest in the areas that will bear the most fruit.

The limits I most often see are actually around conflicting priorities within the school and/or district. By having many different emphases, goals, and strategies, we tend to overload teachers with many competing initiatives. This means that they have much less capacity when it comes to choosing their own professional learning. When their collaborative planning time is overtaken by meetings absent of student work, it is very difficult for them to make their own time for relevant learning.

So, we must find better ways of supporting the time that they do have. We must find asynchronous collaboration points. We must find off-hour times that do not disrupt their family life. Teachers have the capacity to change, each and every year. But only if they are given time and the reason to do so.

There are teachers who have planning times that align across the district, but they would never know it without sharing this capacity with one another. By doing so, it empowers them to reach out via Hangout on a regular basis for questions and answers.

There are teachers who answer email late into the evening, but many times it is the same answer to the same email that was answered a month ago or last year. With a collaborative inbox in Google Groups, they can save those answers and continue to come back to them collectively. They can specifically email to this inbox with their questions, and all of those questions are searchable and linked so that the moderators and members can both play the part of experts as they continue to expand upon ongoing discussions that are already 57 messages deep.

There are teachers who learn best in little snippets while waiting in line at the bank or in the moment after school before they have to pick up their own children. By providing high quality videos in a #2minPD format, they can take advantage of learning opportunities when they have the capacity to do so.

For me, capacity isn't so much about the limitations that time and school/district priorities allow for. Rather, it is much more about understanding where a teacher comes from and how they learn and grow best. When we have this understanding, the support comes easily. When we do not, we have unrealistic expectations for teachers and our PD is met with resistance and disdain.

The Professional Learning Profile is something that helps me see teachers more clearly, and provide supports that better match teachers where they are. However, it is the collaborative process of creating this profile and maintaining it that the most growth happens.

Self-Reflection

Wordpress.com, Blogger.com, or Tumblr.com - Blogging is, quite simply, the best way to reflect upon your practice and show growth over time. It is the gateway drug toward reflective practice. Really, it doesn't matter which tool you choose, so long as you keep a professional portfolio (of sorts) on a blog that continues to grow with you as you learn your craft.

Great Use Cases:
◊ A hub for all of your professional learning (holding all of your resources and tools)
◊ A book club
◊ A series of flipped lesson plans or PD experiences

Vine.co - If you have 6 seconds to spare between classes or after school, you have 6 seconds to share your story and reflect upon it. In fact, I recorded over 103 of them in the course of an afternoon. It served as a keynote for the K-12 Online conference in the process (bit.ly/personalizedpd30).

Great Use Cases:
◊ Messages to yourself about what you want to do better next time.
◊ Quick "teachable moments" that you want to capture from your lesson.
◊ Asking quick questions that push your practice.

Youtube.com - This is a community space that really does thrive on reflection and learning. There are thousands of Educators posting videos every day.

Great Use Cases:
◊ A Daily/Weekly/Monthly Video Blog chronicling your classroom's progress like **Nicholas Provenzano** (bit.ly/personalizedpd32)
◊ A series of walking reflections about big educational questions like **Darren Kuropatwa** (bit.ly/personalizedpd34)
◊ A weekly science video that reaches over a quarter million people like **Paul Andersen** (bit.ly/personalizedpd36)

> **Notegraphy.com** - Part of reflecting is in choosing how to tell your story. I highly recommend using Notegraphy to design just how you want that story to be told. This particular tool lets you reflect using typography and it focuses on short reflections, much like Twitter.
>
> <u>Great Use Cases</u>:
> ◊ Important quotes worth remembering
> ◊ Important questions worth proposing
> ◊ Important learning experiences worth documenting

I have been blogging since my first year of teaching. That sounds much more self-important and revolutionary than it actually is. Many teachers keep a record of their teaching. They write in lesson plan books or they keep a diary of their exploits in the classroom. The only difference was that I put mine online. It is in this simple act of sharing that my work bent toward reflection. Each blog post was not only for my kids, but also for the adults who used my work as a resource. Each link I posted was not just about information sharing, but rather about reflecting upon the value of that information and how much of it was going to last beyond the fifty minute period I had planned.

In a lot of ways that is what I am doing now. I am continuing to share resources widely, and continuing to reflect upon their value. Only this time, the sharing includes not only text and images, but also video. And it is through video that I have found the most concrete evidence of change. It is through the putting of oneself on camera that you truly find out what "capturing" learning is all about.

For me, there are four types of video that help teachers to reflect upon their practice:
1. Reflective Practice Video Blogging: In this video type, teachers can simply talk into the camera about their lessons. They share what is going well and what is really not working. They are open and ask lots of questions. They also encourage feedback and support from their community.
2. Classroom Capture: In this video type, teachers are recording their live classroom so that they can look back on it to analyze and reflect upon their teaching process. They can look at very specific

aspects of their classroom and find out higher impact moves to pursue for next time.

3. Recorded Video Conferences: While we talk about the powerful collaboration that can happen across schools and between teachers, we rarely capture it as it is happening. By recording a video conference, you are much better able to reflect upon your own ability to collaborate and shift practice through conversation.

4. Flipped Lessons: In this video type, teachers are able to share the core of their lessons. While these may be out of the context of time with students, they help support the student work and they help support the teacher making their lessons better by sharing them and getting feedback.

I want to emphasize that it isn't simply the act of *creating* these videos that makes for a shift in practice, but rather the act of *sharing* them.

As a part of my role in Denver, we have created an initiative called Project Cam Opener which aims to open classrooms and schools through video collaborations. In this project we gave 85 teachers a webcam and a microphone in order to engage in the creation of the video types above. While we weren't entirely sure what the videos would look like at the outset, we knew that giving teachers the choice and opportunity would bring about great things for their classrooms. We were right.

Teachers have been innovatively capturing student work by strapping GoPro cameras to helmets and letting kids go about their learning. Teachers have been sharing bilingual classrooms that many other teachers have never had the pleasure of seeing. Teachers have also been simply sitting behind the camera and recording themselves going through their thinking process and voicing their concerns about curriculum choices and teaching strategies.

But these videos weren't just released out into the abyss of the internet. Rather, they were shared with the carefully curated community of other Project Cam Opener participants. That is essential. It is through this community that the feedback happens. It is through this community that encouragement and growth is attainable. While many of the early adopters of these mediums were able to create their own communities, it is up to us as professional developers to ensure that everyone has this kind of a community to share within.

Conclusion

None of this is easy, and it certainly didn't come just from me writing a job description. However, having the ability to see this through from inception to implementation is something I wouldn't trade for the world. If we are truly to revolutionize PD, we must feel free to reinvent our own roles and how we think about what our daily work should be.

We must be free to break down the walls of the one-room schoolhouses throughout our districts. We must see teachers as themselves, their whole selves. We can't see the 100 teachers in a high school as having the same path through a particular initiative, just like we don't see that for our students. We have to use their own capacities for change rather than forcing it upon them when we believe they are ready.

And, we can't wait for others to give us permission or for others to come up with the jobs that will reinvent teaching and learning. We are the ones we have been waiting for, and this is the work that will get us there. We *will* start talking about communities instead of content. We *will* start personalizing our events to the needs, strengths, interests, and capacities of teachers. We *will* start empowering others to use self-reflection in order to drive change.

Ben Wilkoff is the Director of Personalized Professional Learning in Denver Public Schools. He has taught middle schoolers English. He has managed online communities for Edmodo and been an Online Learning and Technology Resources Specialist for Douglas County Schools. He was named the Totally Wired Teacher of the Year in 2007 by Edutopia and has blogged at Learning is Change *since 2004. He is married to his favorite person, and loves his three children quite a little bit. He is passionate about personalized learning, technology with purpose, and creating at least one new thing every day. In short, he teaches, and learns. A lot.*

Twitter: @bhwilkoff
Email: ben@learningischange.com
benjamin_wilkoff@dpsk12.org

146

What is Augmented Reality?
Brad Waid

Augmented reality, or 4D, allows you to bring learning to life by bringing experiences into the classroom that before were impossible, like an exploration of the planets in our solar system or the human heart. Additionally, it allows you to personalize learning for students, teachers, and administrators.

In addition to using augmented reality apps on devices, you can open up your imagination and use an augmented reality creation tool, like DAQRI's 4D Studio (bit.ly/personalizedpd38), to create your own experiences to personalize professional development, duplicate teaching moments, train teachers or students for specific outcomes, and much more.

By creating your own experiences, you can customize your message or your learning outcomes for students or teachers and connect them to a target (the image you scan with your phone or device). This allows them to learn at their own pace and review content as often as needed to maximize learning and fit the pace of the learner.

For example, let's imagine that a day of professional development has five outcomes, and you have five stations for staff to work at throughout the day. Each station would have a target image that has a video, instructions, 3D model, or animation for the learning outcome, and the staff can all interact and review the content as much as is necessary at their own pace. The staff can now work independently or collaboratively to obtain each desired outcome.

Augmented reality is an amazing new medium that brings new dimensions to learning and allows us to bring things into the classroom and the learning environment that we used to only dream about. It is changing the educational landscape, not only for the students in the classroom, but all students, teachers, and administrators on a global scale. It is changing the fundamental way we interact with the world around us and how we learn within our environment.

Brad Waid *is an energetic and passionate educator who inspires educational change through technology and augmented reality. He is a highly sought after international speaker who engages his audience with his passion, humor, mind-blowing demonstrations all while sharing the power of technology and how it can transform the way we learn, teach and lead. He is an industry leader in educational technology and in augmented reality. Brad is an expert in applying technology into the educational field and is on the leading edge of emerging technologies. He is one of the co-founders of AR Detroit, a monthly meetup where industry leaders and visionaries come together to talk about the application and future of augmented reality. Brad is also the co-founder of* Two Guys and Some iPads *blog, an internationally-viewed blog from over 120 countries and over 100,000 visitors in the first four months of its creation. In addition, he is the co-host of the wildly popular and number one rated* Two Guys Show *on the EdReach Network.*

Twitter: @TechBradWaid
Website: twoguysandsomeipads.com

I Want My Own PD
Brad Currie

There is no doubt that we live in one of the most exciting times in education. With all the available technologies and web tools available for professional growth purposes, it's easy for educators to be inspired and frustrated simultaneously. How can this be possible? Easy. Often educators are put in an awkward situation where they are being force-fed professional development because of some state- or district-based mandate. Quite frankly, this helps no one and wastes a whole lot of time and money. The ideal situation would be to ensure educators are offered opportunities to grow how they want, where they want, on what they want, and with whom they want. The solution to innovative and relevant professional development is right in front of our faces. Schools must leverage the power of technology, social media, and Web 2.0 tools to provide anytime and anywhere learning for staff. The increased exposure educators will have to best practices will lead to more student success in the long run.

The one-size-fits-all approach towards growing professionally is slowly being replaced by a more personalized approach that will, in turn, directly impact the success of students. In reality we all know that when districts force learning opportunities upon their staff members, it is counter-productive and unlikely to impact students in any way, shape, or form. From my work with various staff members at my school, the preferred choice for professional development is obvious: allow for professional choice. Personally, I am invigorated more when I can learn about something that interests me and will ultimately contribute to an innovative learning environment. In fact, many of the staff members I work with see it the same way.

In order to better understand how to make flipped professional development work, one must understand all of the available options to those involved in education today. Throughout this chapter, I hope to share some ideas on how I model personalized professional development in my district and school. As a connected educator, some would say I'm modeling for an even larger audience. Perhaps for educators throughout the world.

Quite frankly, traditional professional development has become too one-size-fits-all and does not tap into people's interest. That is why it is essential that educators from all walks of life explore the *flipped* approach to growing professionally. It enables people to take ownership in how they improve their own craft. With all the available technology and web tools, it is no longer an option to stand idly by waiting for best practice resources and methods. Guiding your own learning is a necessity now and will go a long way in promoting the success of all students.

Innovative professional development concepts such as the EdCamp movement, smackdowns, Twitter, hashtags, webinars, online book talks, Google Hangouts, and Walkie Talkie PD directly correlate to a major shift in the way educators evolve in the twenty-first century.

Edcamps
The rise of the EdCamp movement here in the U.S. and abroad is one that will only continue to grow stronger. Educators are meeting up in various locations and can share or learn what they want. It's an incredibly informal process that provides participants the freedom to collaborate, share, and learn about best practices in education. EdCamps are totally free to attend and often provide you with breakfast and lunch. (You can find your local EdCamp and learn how to start one by visiting edcamp.org.)

An Edcamp is an educational unconference where participants learn and share what they want, how they want. Upon arrival participants will see a session board where they can sign up to hold a discussion or simply take in their options. The thrust behind EdCamps is an environment based on discussion rather presentation. For example, if you are attending a session on using Google Apps in the classroom, and it does not interest you because your school is 1:1 with iPads, simply get up out of your seat, walk out, and find a session related to your interests. This is a great example of flipped PD simply because you are taking ownership of your own professional growth. It's not being dictated to you by a large educational conference's predetermined schedule. If you walk down the hall to another room, you may experience a conversation that is taking place on how to start a MakerSpace or how to flip your faculty meeting.

That's the greatness about EdCamps; participants vote with their two feet. It might seem unconventional, but if you really think about it, the impact this can have on professional growth is a game-changer. How, you might ask? Simple. When people are given the autonomy to learn and share it opens up the door for innovation and a relevant learning environment. I have personally come away with ideas that were instantly implemented into my school related to such best practices as branding, Google Apps, 1:1 implementation, and body language.

Many educators have been so inspired by the EdCamp experience that they have started their own within their school or district. It seems like a perfect solution to the age-old question "What do we do for our staff in-service day?" Having staff hold conversations on what they are passionate about in education is the key to professional growth. The bottom line is that EdCamps are free of charge, and the networking connections you will make will have an impact on who you are as an educator.

Over the past few years, I have personally attended a handful of EdCamps such as EdCamp Leadership, EdCampNJ, and PadCamp. (Learn more about each of these great professional growth opportunities here: edcampleadership.org; edcampnj.org; padcamp.org.) All were very valuable and well worth the time commitment. Simply put, there is no reason not to attend an EdCamp in order to see all that is right with innovative professional development. The sharing and, more importantly, the connections that are made are priceless. Most EdCamps conclude with a smackdown, a thirty-minute session of apps, websites, and other online resources shared and explained as they relate to application in the classroom setting. As an added bonus, one of the EdCamp organizers will archive the resources and share on a web-based spreadsheet for future use.

Smackdowns

Have you ever been apart of a sharing session in school or at an educational conference that turns your world upside down? A few years ago at the end of EdCampNJ, attendees came up to the big screen and shared their favorite web-based resources. Participants highlighted and explained tools for assessment, the backchannel, curation, communication, collaboration, and creation in a quick, yet efficient manner. Organizers of the event archived the resources shared on a spreadsheet so that attendees could refer back to them at a later date. Digitizing resources via Google Drive or other web-based applications enables sharing to be that much more powerful. Seeing the power of a smackdown in action was truly remarkable and inspired me to conduct one at my next faculty meeting.

In the week leading up to one of our faculty meetings, I gave our teachers a heads-up that there would be a sharing session. During the last ten minutes of the meeting, staff members would walk up to the laptop connected to a projector and share an edtech website they use in class. While this was happening, I archived the resources on to a spreadsheet so that our staff could go and explore them more at a later time. It's really amazing just how many innovative web-based tools teachers are using. I truly believe the more we share, the more of an impact we will all have on students.

For example, one of the resources that was shared at our faculty meeting smackdown was Newsela (newsela.com), an innovative way to build reading comprehension through current event articles. Each article is available at five different reading levels and is Common Core aligned. One of our teachers soon thereafter infused the tool in her 8th grade language arts class. Students were able to select articles on their devices aligned to the book they were reading at the time. The combination of technology integration and high-interest reading material provided students with a tremendous learning experience. Fortunately, our entire staff at Black River School in Chester, NJ, loves to share best practices knowing that in the long run, it helps promote the success of all students.

Twitter

There is great excitement in education today due in large part to educators being able to connect online and share best practices with tools like Twitter, a form of micro-blogging that allows users to push out content in 140 characters or less. It's your one-stop online shopping experience chock full of connections to the best minds in the business and useful content that will help you grow as a professional. I can tell you unequivocally that my time as a connected educator on Twitter and the many opportunities I have to learn from my PLN has changed my professional life for the better.

Through Twitter, users can easily share links, videos, and pictures. Have a question that you need an answer to? No problem. Just tweet it out, and I guarantee somebody will get back to you with an answer. Twitter also serves as a wonderful search engine. Simply type in whatever it is that you are looking for and hundreds of tweets will appear with relevant information. Looking to promote your classroom or school happenings? Twitter can prove wonders in telling your story, informing stakeholders, and promoting all that is good.

As you can see it is definitely one of the most exciting times to be in education. Twitter provides educators with so many options to better themselves. It's no longer an option to be connected and take advantage of all that is being shared in the virtual world. The playing field has been leveled, and sharing is no longer a taboo. The more educators connect and share using a tool like Twitter, the better chance student success will be impacted in ways once thought unimaginable.

Hashtags
The word "hashtag" was recently added to the dictionary and has revolutionized the way people share, organize, and archive information on social media sites. Basically when a user posts a comment or link on a social media site they include a hashtag. It provides relevance and archives a post within a certain thread. One hashtag in particular, #satchat, is near and dear to my heart. It has given me an opportunity to connect with current and emerging school leaders in the wonderful world of Twitter. Each and every Saturday morning at 7:30 ET, educators use the #satchat hashtag in their tweets to share ideas and resources related to the discussion topic. Throughout the week when the actual discussion is not taking place, educators will use the #satchat hashtag to gain access to timely information and best practice links. For example, to find a leadership resource on Twitter simply type in the #satchat hashtag in the search box. In a recent #satchat discussion on EdCamps, participants shared their experiences and what it was like to attend. It was amazing the amount of people who had not yet been to an

EdCamp and how inspired they now were to either start their own or attend one in person. The #satchat hashtag has been powerful sharing tool for educators and has flattened the educational world for the better. Hashtags have enabled educators to customize their learning when they want and how they want. There are subject specific hashtags and more general hashtags that deal with such topics as leadership.

A great starting point for using the most relevant hashtags would be to check out Jerry Blumengarten's webpage on Twitter: cybraryman.com/twitter.html. There are so many hashtags to follow in education that all you need to do to start by thinking about your role in education. Are you a school leader? Try out #satchat and #PersonalizedPD. A parent? Check out #ptchat (Parent-Teacher). Educational junkie? No doubt you will love #edchat. Addicted to educational technology? Follow #edtech and #edtechchat. I could go on and on. Whether it's a state-oriented hashtag, like #iaedchat (Iowa), #njed (New Jersey), or #arkedchat (Arkansas), or a subject-specific hashtag such as #sschat (Social Studies), you have so many options at your fingertips. Emerging best practice teaching trend hashtags such as #flipclass provide users a venue to consume and be inspired to take risks in the classroom.

The great thing about hashtags is that they are applicable to a number of social media sites. Using your search box feature will help with finding resources related to a particular hashtag. Instagram, for example, is an outstanding app for visual learners. A very popular hashtag educators use to share and gain access to ideas in the form of pictures is #teachersfollowteachers. Whether you are looking for a bulletin board idea or want to see what a particular learning experience looks like in the classroom setting, Instagram provides educators with an opportunity to grow in ways once thought unimaginable. To actually see a class of students through pictures participating in a problem-based learning activity, for example, can give educators a view of how a lesson would look in various stages.

One of the main advantages of flipping your professional development in the virtual world is that you are able to connect with educators from around the world. The more educators share best practices, the more student success will be impacted. Whether it's learning how to integrate primary source documents into your lessons or revamping your classroom to foster a more collaborative learning environment, the connected world is the place to be.

Online Book Talks
Online book talks are making an impact on how educators learn and connect with each other on a global basis. Basically, a group of people will come together online using a website such as Edmodo and post their comments related to a book they are reading. The conversation typically takes place in a question/answer format and can last for a month or two. In 2013, I was fortunate enough to lead a district-wide Edmodo book talk on Dave Burgess' *Teach Like a Pirate* (The online book talk that focused on this book would never have happened if it weren't for Twitter #tlap). Staff members signed up for an Edmodo account at edmodo.com and over a two-month period shared their insight on passion-based teaching and resources to support their thinking. Interested in taking part in an online book talk? Look no further than your PLN. Put the questions out there on social media and you are sure to find one taking place on Edmodo, Twitter, Voxer, Google+, or Facebook. These virtual discussion groups are sometimes very large with over 1000 participants, other times they could contain fewer than ten.

Because of its effectiveness in an educational setting, we chose Edmodo as the tool for the online book talk. Edmodo is a web-based learning management system that enables teachers and students to hold a virtual classroom of sorts. Assignments, links, videos, and other materials can be posted and commented on in a secure setting. Because of the online environment for the book talk, we were able to bring Dave Burgess into the discussion. It's not often that you get to have the author of a book share insight. The entire experience allowed everyone to reflect on their experiences in the classroom. The connection I had with Dave on Twitter provided me an opportunity to approach him about participating. Without hesitation, he obliged and was so gracious with his time during the two-month chat. Through email and direct messages on Twitter, I was able to schedule times for Dave to participate. Many authors, including myself, are very eager to participate in online book discussions or Twitter chats. Simply send them a tweet or email, and they usually contact you with available times.

In 2014, I was again put in the fortunate position to help run another Edmodo book talk, with fellow #satchat moderators Scott Rocco and Billy Krakower, focusing on Eric Sheninger's book *Digital Leadership*. In this particular instance over 175 educators from around the world shared their insight on best practices as it related to leading and learning in the digital era. In the weeks leading up to the chat, we promoted the concept on Twitter using the #satchat hashtag and gained tremendous interest. Participants would comment on questions posted primarily by Billy in the Edmodo group. As an added bonus, Eric Sheninger himself participated in the chat and shed light on his journey as a digital leader. The comments and resources posted during this online discussion (see below) gave me, as well as others, an opportunity to reflect and gain insight on what is possible in education.

Jennifer Priddy to ■ Digital Leadership - Chapter 7 (2014 #Satchat Book Discussion)

Q20: What message do you want to resonate with your stakeholders?
I would want stakeholders to know that we feel ALL students can learn and this is how our school is meeting the needs of every student. I would want them to know how we differentiate learning and how we are teaching to the 21st century student. I would also want stakeholders to feel a part of what is happening in our schools.

Q21: How to you create and sustain both a positive brand presence for your school and at the individual level? One word: PRIDE. I think creating a school climate where staff,...
Show Full Post

⊙ ∨ · ○ Reply · ☑ Share   Jun 24, 2014

Jennifer Priddy to ■ Digital Leadership - Chapter 6 (2014 #Satchat Book Discussion)

Q16: How can you take control of public relations to become the storyteller-in-chief? Why does this even matter?
I haven't had an opportunity to take control of a school's story given that I have been unemployed for 7 years. However, at my son's school, great news is shared often in the local newspaper. Also, the PTO has a FB page, too, but that is underutilized, in my opinion. I intend on advocating my future school's story through Twitter and FB, if I am able. This is important because our stakeholders want to know! All stakeholders should have...
Show Full Post

The online book talk is a great example of flipping the way educators grow as professionals. Typically in a traditional book talk, a group of people are in a room and discuss chapters based on their insight. Making the discussion virtual allows for more global perspective on educational issues and allows conversations to take place in real-time or at your own pace.

Walkie-Talkie PD

Did you ever think there would be a time in the history of education where educators from all walks of life could turn their mobile device into a walkie-talkie strictly for professional development purposes? Neither did I. That is, of course, until an app called Voxer made its way onto the educational scene (voxer.com). The concept is very simple. Download the Voxer app onto your device, set up an account, find like-minded people you want to connect with, and share best practice ideas in a "vox" or what some call a chat room. Anytime a great thought or educational topic comes up that you would like to discuss, simply tap the push to talk button and leave a message with the person or group you are chatting with. The person(s) on the other end will listen to your message and reply accordingly. Voxer works in the same way as text messaging in terms of how you can share links and ideas in a text box. This is such a revolutionary tool for educators because it puts a voice with the name. For example, I was fortunate enough to be named to the 2014 ASCD Emerging Leaders Class. I met so many great people and wanted to continue learning from them in the month and years to come. I set up a Voxer group with these tremendous leaders in order to stay in touch and continue sharing best practices.

The concept is quite remarkable of how a walkie-talkie conversation can change the face of professional growth. The aforementioned book talk on Sheninger's *Digital Leadership* actually took place through Voxer. We would leave voice message reflections and share ideas pertaining to the topics that were raised. To be honest, it felt weird at first, but over time it became abundantly clear that the insight being shared through voice messages was having a profound impact on my beliefs as an educator. Better yet, as we participated in this walkie-talkie discussion, best practice resources were shared in the form of websites and pictures that supplemented our discussion points. If you want to join a group discussion on Voxer, contact the organizer through email or Twitter and they will add you to the conversation. #satchat has formed its own Voxer group and provides participants a chance to extend Saturday's conversation for the entire week on various educational topics. Twitter participants can contact me and ask to be added to the Voxer. Each day, I post a discussion point where people can share their insight through a "vox" or voice message.

Moving forward there is no doubt that web-based applications such as Voxer will leave a positive mark on the educational landscape, simply because people learn in so many different ways. Whether it's visually, orally, virtually, physically, or by just reading a blog post, educators need to make sense of the world they work in through what they feel comfortable with. Tools like Voxer could also be used for communication and learning with students as well. Wouldn't it be neat if students could create their own vox in order to show what they know about a given topic? Fellow PLN member Jenny Grabiec suggested that, during the summer months, Voxer could be used as a tech help line (brilliant idea!) to assist those with technology integration questions or suggestions. The options are limitless and go a long way in helping educators grow and stay on top of their A-game.

Webinars
Picture it. After a long day of work, a teacher sits at her desk exhausted from a tremendous day of leading young learners through a series of hands-on learning experiences. She is happy, but not satisfied with how the lesson impacted student's ability to comprehend the topic at hand. Understanding the importance of improving her craft in order to seek out more innovative methods to reach students, she receives an email promoting an upcoming webinar on integrating iPads to engage learners in authentic learning experiences. Later on that week, she takes it upon herself to watch the webinar and ultimately infuses some of the ideas shared. The students love the new ways they are learning about concepts through the various iPad apps. This is just another example of how educators flip their own learning through leveraging the power of webinars to grow on their own time.

Over the past five years, webinars have really become a mainstay in the educational world. Educators can learn about a variety of topics on their own time via streaming video. Whether it's technology integration, differentiated instruction, or classroom management, there is a plethora of ways to stay on top of best practices in the virtual world. Some of the top names in the business conduct webinars for free or at very little cost. With the evolution of connected educators sharing best practice ideas on social media, they have also now turned to webinars to share their knowledge. For those who are interested in educational apps, I strongly encourage you to check out Monica Burn's (@ClassTechTips) webinars on *Simple K12*. The vast knowledge she has about specific apps that activate student engagement is truly amazing. If you are looking to get started in your own educational growth through webinars, two companies in particular, EdWeb.net and SimpleK12.com have a robust library of webinars that can help educators grow on their own time.

Google Hangouts and Other Virtual Meetings?

Have you ever wanted live access to an educator or group of educators in order to converse about a question you have or to share best practices? Google Hangouts allow this to be a reality. With a few clicks, educators from around the world can see and talk to each other on the computer screen in real time. Whether it's planning an event, conducting an interview, or simply sharing an idea that could make a good lesson great, Google Hangouts are the way to go. For me personally, I am able to have fulfilling conversations with people when seeing each other through a Google Hangout. It almost feels like you are having a conversation with the other person in the flesh. Emailing or calling someone on the phone is one thing, but to connect and actually see the person is truly amazing. Often when people are able to interact with other people virtually while actually seeing each other builds a deeper connection on many fronts. It personalizes the learning experience and enables people to truly understand what is being discussed.

So how can a Google Hangout be beneficial towards your professional development? Speaking from first-hand experience, the benefits are many. Over the past few years, I have conducted Google Hangouts with educators from around the country. Take for example the virtual show Starr Sackstein and I record on Google Hangout called Ed Perspectives. Starr, a teacher in New York City, and I hold an engaging discussion on a wide variety of educational topics from standardized testing to effective lesson planning. As this conversation takes place, it's being recorded on a computer via Google Hangout OnAir. Once the session is complete, we upload it to YouTube for all to enjoy. The experience gives us and the viewers a chance to reflect on our beliefs as it pertains to educational issues. You can learn more about these sessions by visiting Starr's website at starrsackstein.com. I know of schools that will bring in a keynote speaker or author during their faculty meeting by way of a Google Hangout. The insight shared during a Hangout can do wonders for ultimately impacting the success of all students.

Not a big fan of Google Hangouts? No problem. Try another Voice Over Internet Protocol (VOIP) such as Skype or FaceTime to connect, see, hear, and learn from each other in real time. I can remember Skyping with Eric Sheninger on one occasion. He had just read one of my blog posts and wanted to share his thoughts. Having instant visual access to a great educational technology leader such as Eric was tremendous, to say the least. I can remember another occasion when Maggie Bolado, an educator from Texas, wanted to chat about school hashtags and digital newsletters in the school setting. We decided to conduct our conversation on a Google Hangout. I was so inspired by what Maggie was doing in her classroom and school that I decided to start a digital newsletter to keep our school stakeholders informed of school happenings. Examples like the two above are proof of the power of being a connected educator. Being actively involved in personal learning networks provides people with an opportunity to seek out advice and reflect. On another occasion, I can recall using FaceTime on my iPhone to speak with Diana Potts' 4th grade class during a Mystery Location Call. A mystery location call is when students had to guess where in the world I was calling from based on the answers I gave to their questions. The lessons learned from this experience will most definitely last for a lifetime. How powerful it is that at any given moment you can tap on your device and have a real-life, face-to-face conversation about best practices with an educator from another part of the country or world? There is no doubt that the evolution of video messaging has transformed the educational landscape.

The Changing Face of Educational Conferences

For a time, educational conferences were hit and miss as it relates to having a profound impact on professional growth. Recently, however, social media has been a game-changer in how people connect and learn both in a physical and virtual sense. Gone are the days that a person has to be in attendance to actually gain insight from an educational conference. Twitter has enabled educators to follow the conference hashtag where attendees can post content from a session they are attending. Take for example the NASSP (National Association of Secondary School Principals) Ignite Conference. Every year, thousands of secondary school leaders converge at a given location to attend the conference. But what about the countless others that weren't able to make it? No problem. Simply hop onto Twitter, type in the conference hashtag, and follow participant tweets from the many wonderful sessions. It's a great way to stay connected and learn from some of the best minds in education. In addition, conferences have live streaming sessions that people can watch from home or at work. There are so many ways to develop yourself professionally from an educational conference without actually being there.

The evolution of social media has also changed the way attendees interact with each other at conferences. In the past you would attend a conference possibly knowing a handful of people and sharing a few ideas. Fast forward to the present and you will experience a much different environment. Attendees show up and greet each other like they have been friends forever. Ideas and resources are shared with ease due to the fact that the initial awkward barrier has been eliminated due to the relationship they have using a tool like Twitter. The bottom line is that being a connected educator in the both the physical and virtual world has so many benefits that ultimately impact the success of students.

As you can see, there are so many ways to grow as an educator given the vast amount of resources in today's society. Whether it's through a hashtag on Twitter or attending a local EdCamp, the options are limitless. There is no doubt that there is value in reading an educational magazine and that it can have an impact on your growth as an educator. However, in my opinion, there is much more to gain from the vast online edtech tools of today. Technology has transformed the way educators can personalize their learning experience 24/7, 365 days a year. Taking ownership of your own professional growth can happen now quickly online. Learning about and sharing best practices in the virtual world and physical world, when the opportunity arises, is a win-win for all school stakeholders and solidifies our commitment to doing what's best for kids.

Brad Currie *is the Supervisor of Instruction and Dean of Students for the Chester School District in Chester, New Jersey. He is the founding partner of Evolving Educators, LLC (evolvingeducators.com).*

Brad is the author of All Hands on Deck: Tools for Connecting Educators, Parents, and Communities *(corwin.com/books/Book244207).*

He is an ASCD Emerging Leader and Certified Google Trainer. Brad is the co-founder and co-moderator of an online Twitter discussion for current and emerging school leaders called #Satchat.

Twitter: @bradmcurrie
Website: bradcurrie.net

What are TeachMeets?

Dr. Matthew Martin

TeachMeets are a grass-roots, professional development phenomenon currently being organised by teachers and for teachers in roughly a dozen countries around the world. They originated in Scotland in 2006 but have now spread to Canada, the US, Ireland, Denmark, the Czech Republic, and a handful of other countries.

Organised and run entirely by teachers, these events are characterised by a non-hierarchical structure more closely akin to that of a flash mob rather than a formal conference. Arrangements are made through wikis, Twitter, and Facebook to convene a TeachMeet in a given area. (The location changes regularly so as to ensure all have easy access.)

Teachers are then asked to register by ordering a free e-ticket online. When registering, teachers may also indicate whether they have an effective idea, a teaching method, or a resource which they are using currently and would like to present to the group. At the event, all the names of potential presenters are put into a random name generator and teachers are called up to speak in no particular order and with no guarantee that everyone will be called.

Teachers are asked, 'Would you like to deliver a 'long' talk or a 'short' talk?' 'Long' talks are seven minutes and 'short' talks are two minutes. A moderator is usually on hand with a stopwatch to keep things moving at a brisk pace. The effect of these arrangements – the short talks and the unpredictable speaking order – is to produce an atmosphere of considered spontaneity. In other words, some people have come prepared to speak. They might have PowerPoint presentations on a memory stick or notes in hand, but they most likely have not laboured endlessly over their talk, knowing all along, as they have, that their name may never be called.

With most talks lasting two minutes, the mission of the evening is clearly to get core ideas across quickly and sensibly, just as one might when telling a friend over coffee. At the end of a TeachMeet, then, those attending will have been exposed to a large number of new ideas and introduced to a large number of creative, committed practitioners whom they will be able to speak to during the break should their interests overlap.

In every locale, TeachMeets have their own impetus and respond to the needs of their immediate context. Here in Northern Ireland, where I recently helped to organise one, the context has been quite specifically one of a radically changing curriculum.

"Northern Ireland has recently rolled out a new 'Revised Curriculum' across the primary and secondary sectors," says Daithí Murray, one of the founders of the Northern Ireland TeachMeet movement. "The new curriculum raised everyone's sights in relation to our ambitions in schools and got us talking more holistically about helping students to develop as individuals, to use their thinking and problem-solving skills to contribute to society, and to develop their creativity and self-management.

"And yet," says Murray, "frustration was rife among teachers about the professional development opportunities available to us in this new curricular context. Our experience was of days out on courses which were only as good as the person running them – and which seemed to vary in terms of the facilitator's own experience and commitment to the ideas at stake. Social media, and Twitter particularly, allowed us for the first time – as these ideas echoed and grew in the twittersphere – to realise, in that oft-quoted phrase, that 'we are the people we have been waiting for.' We came to believe in our own ability to push our own professional development forward.

"There is room for much research around this movement, as we cannot currently point to evidence of its efficacy. We are not peer-reviewed or institutionally managed. But we have surveys of participants speaking powerfully about its energising and enabling effects on current teaching practice. And that is always the target– to enable, empower, and energise the teaching that is actually happening out on the ground."

Oh, and TeachMeets are fun, I might add. 'Fun' might even be a definitive characteristic of the TeachMeet approach to the professional development of educators. They usually have food and prizes and raffles. At the very least, fun is a hugely important by-product of the enterprise. The first TeachMeet I ever attended was more than fun; it was exhilarating. The energy and atmosphere generated by the speed and good humour of all involved made it feel like no other conference I had attended.

TeachMeets have been referred to as the 'speed dating' of teacher professional development, and the comparison is rather an apt one. Perhaps some of what you encounter on the night will not be of interest, but you know it's likely to pass quickly, and something new will be along in a couple of minutes.

When I agreed to host a Northern Ireland TeachMeet in my institution (St Mary's University College, Belfast), word came through pretty quickly that the date chosen happened to be the same as the planned upcoming teachers' strike. Nonetheless, ticket 'sales' for the TeachMeet continued to exceed all expectations. When those registered were contacted and asked if the strike would affect their attendance, one teacher replied, 'No, TeachMeets aren't work.' And that divide seems to hold.

TeachMeets connect with teachers' love of teaching, their love of helping and inspiring young people. They manage to create a space which keeps the bureaucratic pressures surrounding the profession today in reasonable perspective. They manage to be freeing yet purposeful, fun yet professional, considered yet spontaneous. They seem to point the way to a new future of teacher professional development in Northern Ireland.

To find out more about the Northern Ireland TeachMeet movement and to make contact with the community, please go to: tmbelfast.wikispaces.com and follow @tmbelfast

*Dr. **Matthew Martin** is Senior Lecturer in English at St Mary's University College, Belfast, Northern Ireland, where he lectures on the Bachelor of Education degree and the BA in Liberal Arts degree. He has taught at the primary and secondary levels and is currently Team Leader for Dissemination in the St Mary's Centre for Excellence in Teaching and Learning. It is in this capacity that he has helped to develop writing programmes and writing centres at a number of other higher education institutions throughout the UK and Ireland.*

Twitter: @matthewmenglish
Email: matthew.martin@stmarys-belfast.ac.uk

Afterword:
A Push From The PIRATE
Dave Burgess

I have never apologized, backed away from, or held any reservations about declaring teaching to be the mightiest profession in the world. It is the profession from which all others flow. Education is at the very center—the root—of all progress. We are literally life-changers. In *Teach Like a PIRATE* I wrote, "We are superheroes wearing the Clark Kent disguise of teacher," and my opinion has only been strengthened and validated by what I have seen as I travel around the educational world.

If we accept, as I do, that teachers are the single biggest determinant of student success in our school systems, then it stands to reason that building their capacity to teach more powerfully, influentially, and effectively is of the utmost importance. Time, money, and energy are finite resources in districts all across the world. Therefore, we need to ask where we can best apply these resources to have the most impact. The answer is simple: professional development. Powerful PD is the Archimedes lever that can move any school or district to the highest levels of success.

The problem is that one-size-fits-all professional development continues to be the norm, even in an educational climate that has moved further and further towards embracing differentiated instruction and personalized learning for students in its classrooms. What about us? If these latest educational innovations have been proven to dramatically increase student learning, then doesn't it make sense that they may increase the learning of educators as well? After all, the best teachers I know are the ones that still see themselves as works in progress and are continually looking for new ways to improve. They are learners. They are students of their profession and calling.

This book is filled to the brim with innovative ways to transform professional development and bring a much-needed variety to the way it is delivered. You may, in fact, be overwhelmed by the sheer quantity of ideas presented here and that sense of overwhelm can lead to "analysis paralysis." I have a suggestion. Just try one thing. That's it...just one thing! After that, try another! It really is that simple, even though we educators love to be professional complicators.

If some of these strategies seem outside of your comfort zone, all the better! That is where all progress is found. I tell teachers all the time that safe lessons are a recipe for mediocrity. The same is true for our professional development. I want to be energized by PD. I want to leave more on fire about my profession. I want to leave feeling more excited about getting back in my classroom and to feel more equipped to do powerful work. Educational leaders have to walk the talk. Don't talk to me about innovation, risk-taking, collaboration, connectedness, and creativity if the professional development you provide models none of this.

Do you want teachers to build innovative, collaborative, and empowering lessons that reach all students in your classrooms? Then start by designing innovative, collaborative, and empowering PD that reaches all teachers. This book is a treasure chest full of those ideas to plunder like a pirate.

Dave Burgess is the New York Times Best-Selling author of Teach Like A PIRATE: Increase Student Engagement, Boost Your Creativity, and Transform Your Life as an Educator and co-author of P is for PIRATE: Inspirational ABC's for Educators. *He is a highly sought-after professional development speaker well-known for his creative, entertaining, and outrageously energetic style. His workshops, seminars, and keynotes not only motivate and inspire teachers, but also help them to develop practical ways to become more creative and engaging in the classroom. Dave empowers teachers to embrace the mighty purpose of being an educator and sparks them to design classes that are life-changing experiences for students. Dave specializes in teaching hard-to-reach, hard-to-motivate students with techniques that incorporate showmanship and creativity.*

Twitter: @burgessdave
Website: DaveBurgess.com

Explanatory

These chapters include many, *many* references to websites, tools, mobile apps, and their associated companies. While most of them are trademarked names, we did not wish to plague our readers with a plethora of ™ symbols throughout. All such names are the sole property of their respective companies, and are referenced here only because they have been of value to the educator-authors who mention them.

Please be sure to explore all of the websites we shared in the book including the shortened links we customized using bitly.com Though we have included many links, it is the nature of the Internet to change. We have made every effort to ensure that all links are correct and active. In addition, educational technology companies are always updating and improving their services (and/or going out of business), so please realize that while all information is accurate at the time of publication, what you actually experience may change from its original description. Either way, feel free to contact us because we would like to help. Let's keep learning together.

CPSIA information can be obtained at www.ICGtesting.com
Printed in the USA
LVOW10s1628040516

486687LV00016B/751/P